SPAIN

Through the Eyes of a Black American Woman

Joy E. Glenn

Copyright © 2021 by Joy E. Glenn

All rights reserved. No part of this publication may be reproduced, distributed, or transmitted in any form or by any means, including photocopying, recording, or other electronic or mechanical methods, without the prior written permission of the publisher, except in the case of brief quotations embodied in critical reviews and certain other noncommercial uses permitted by copyright law.

To all the people of Spain; good and bad. For without this country, my experiences of this book would not be in existence.

Table of Contents

INTRODUCTION 5

BOOK DESCRIPTION 6

JOY ESTHER GLENN 7

ACKNOWLEDGMENT 8

CHAPTER 1:   WHY SPAIN? 9

CHAPTER 2:   SPAIN THROUGH THE EYES OF MY BLACK AMERICAN CHILDREN 61

CHAPTER 3:   HARMONIOUS BONDS 113

CHAPTER 4:   MY LOVES AND HATES OF SPAIN 166

CHAPTER 5:   EXPLORING SPAIN 199

CHAPTER 6:   WOULD I STAY? 227

CHAPTER 7:   SPAIN THROUGH THE EYES OF MY CAMERA LENS 244

CONTACT PAGE 280

Introduction

The lives in which my family and I established in Spain have been wonderful. I wanted to share these experiences with the world but especially with the people of Spain. I want Spaniards to view their country and culture through my eyes, my words and my stories.

Book Description

Embracing change can be difficult, nevertheless the Glenn family withstood this challenge with open arms, understanding, and gratitude. The question may ring in your minds like a million phones. How will a young Black American family survive in a European country like Spain? Will they adapt? Will they make friends? Will they undergo discrimination as they did in their own country? Will they stay? The answer to all of these questions are exquisitely answered in this beautifully written reality of a young Black American Queen and her family.

Not only are the experiences of Joy E. Glenn being distributed throughout this book, yet those of her husband, children and sisters are shared as well. Each family member evolving through learning a new language (Spanish), embracing the culture and traveling. The family's divine presence in Spain provides healing for each of them individually, yet from different measures. These detailed stories of both favorable and unfavorable accounts possess not only truth but opinions through the eyes of a Black American Woman.

Joy Esther Glenn

Joy E. Glenn is a native of South Florida, USA and a 7-year United States Air Force veteran. She is a wife of 13 years and counting as she and her husband together bore 3 beautiful children. Her past and present life' journeys have transformed her into a spiritual, confident, powerful and humble Queen.

Joy has deployed and lived in 4 different countries: achieving multiple awards and medals throughout her military career. Because of these accomplishments Joy was able to travel the world and channel not only her leadership skills but her writing skills as well. Having knowledge of different cultures, Joy started writing short stories and poetry. Honoring this skill and hobby, she recently decided to produce her first book in 2018.

Acknowledgment

In light of the world's current state; we need God's love and light to be shared. With that being stated, I'd like to first thank God Almighty and His son, Jesus Christ for blessing me with life and purpose. Secondly my amazing earthly king, Amos who has supported me every step of this book journey. To my extraordinary children Amari, Aaron, and Abigail for their sweet love and support that gives me strength. To my powerful sister, Zipporah, who's expertise and word-smith gift have tremendously helped me write this book. Last but certainly not least, thank you to ALL the people of Spain whom have embraced us and abetted us to live this marvelous experience.

Chapter 1:

Why Spain?

Spain was not a country I can remember attesting to the future of my family; however, God saw our time ahead and he chose Spain for us. I can recall many years after coming into my own realizations of the racism in America and the hardships many face just to live a peaceful and average life, how I possessed a sense of urgency to apply for passports for me and my children. My youngest baby girl, Abigail, was only eight weeks of age; Aaron, my middle, was two and a half years; and Amari, my oldest child was six years old. My motherly instinct was telling me to move past my comfort zone and I began to visualize myself in another land other than the one we were all born in.

My husband, Amos, had just completed his last enlistment in the United States Air Force, as did I in 2014. We were both in agreement that we wanted to live abroad as we did in our past during our military careers. Nevertheless, this time living abroad would be largely different because now we could take off the uniform, heal from the pain of being constantly apart due to our military duties, and most importantly continue to broaden the minds and horizons of our three small children together. My brain would often venture into this idea and I would instantly feel a sense of gratitude and excitement. Before moving to Spain, my family and I were living in Navarre, which is the northeast side of Florida, in the United States. We loved the cheaper cost of living and the closeness of the ocean; however, this area like many others in North Florida, lacked diversity, culture and displayed racism. We wanted more and we knew that what we sought was within our reach.

One day Amos arrived home from Atlanta, Georgia, where he recently acquired paid training due to his military background. But the problem we often faced was the constant separation of our family. Amos would be hours if not days away working while I remained home with the children. Not only did this leave a physical strain on the development of our family bond, but it also hindered our spiritual growth because we all wanted and needed Amos home. We did not want to experience division if it was not necessary for the survival of our family. I could discern Amos's spirit and see that he greatly enjoyed his job in Atlanta, yet he enjoyed being home more. He desired something permanent yet without the need to be away from his family. I, after battling depression for many years, being a stay-at-home mother, encountering two pregnancies without Amos, and living in places without my intermediate family, knew in my heart that this was not the way to evolve as a family. As a team Amos and I decided that it would be best for our family if he found a job overseas that could accommodate us all staying together. Amos began his search as we began our prayers. Within the next few months, a job was offered to Amos by an American contracting company. Amos fit all the requirements and qualifications and we knew this was the position for him. Seeing that it was in Spain sparked my excitement and I began preparing mentally for this new adventure, for my faith was larger than a mustard seed and my willpower was stronger than an ox.

As time progressed and we received notice that Amos obtained the job offer, we began preparation mentally, physically, and spiritually. I started Spanish lessons for the children and myself, looked up schools, researched the cost of living and much more. Everything seemed divine and I was ready to embark on this new journey with my family. I could see the future of my children, myself and Amos speaking Spanish fluently, I could imagine swimming on the beaches of southern Spain, but most importantly I saw myself and Amos getting back into our routine of being one again. So, when I am asked "why did I choose Spain," my answer would simply be that I did not choose Spain, but Spain chose us—the Glenns of North Florida—and now we will rise as a tribe knowing that we accomplished this change together.

One unique element of our venture to Spain was that Zipporah, my older sister by one year, decided to come join us. Not only was she coming to live, but she made the conscious decision to bring our niece D'iona along with her. I can recollect the day when we were all discussing the different aspects of Spain and how we would all benefit from stepping out of the negative energy of America to a different country. I was not sure if Zipporah was serious about coming, but I had faith that God would lead her into confidence to make that change with us and join the tribe. I knew it was the will of God because her lease was ending no less than a month after my family's departure, placing her and D'iona's arrival two months after ours. D'iona was excited about the opportunity to live abroad and I knew it would be a sense of healing for her. I thought to myself, she needs the exposure, the bond with Amos and the feeling of having siblings. I must admit that I was nervous knowing I would be mothering another child, but D'iona was like my own; therefore, my nervousness would always just be in passing. Her personality was perfectly webbed into our family's and I felt she was ready. Zipporah and I would talk every week during our preparation to leave America for Spain. She was living in Margate, which is south of Florida and I know she enjoyed her home, but she was also as ready as I was to experience somewhere outside of America. I can recall the times when Zipporah was there during my struggle of being disconnected from Amos due to his job location. We would visit one another from North to South Florida and the bond we built as adults led her into coming along on this journey with us. I needed my sister and my sister needed me. My immediate, intermediate, and in-law family are all very important to my life and growth as a person. They all play a role in my husband's and my family union. We knew we would miss them tremendously, and us them. Nevertheless, we all needed this change, and we were grateful to have it.

 August arrived as fast as Usain Bolt can run. I could not believe my eyes as I stood in my empty house in Navarre, Florida, reminiscing on all the memories that were not only made here in this house but all the memories my family and I made as a union in Florida. Minutes passed and I could see our instruments sitting in the corner, now packed up on the truck. I could hear us singing together, laughing and playing games in this very house. My mind suddenly flashed to the many memories I knew we would make greater in Spain. I then shut off every light, texted Amos that I was leaving to Margate, Florida, to spend time with Zipporah, and Keturah, our oldest sister and mother of D'iona. I shut the door and it was as though I was walking into a portal as I saw myself walking into Spain and welcoming it as my new home.

Arriving in Spain

It was August 23, 2018, and we had arrived. Amos entered Spain a month prior to get acquainted with the area and set up for his new supervisor position on the airbase, which was close to where we would be living. Leaving Florida and arriving in Spain was definitely a difficult task with three small children and my anxiety was at an all-time high during the entire process. However, when I entered the atmosphere of Seville, Spain, where we landed, I felt a gust of peace enter my spirit and I heard the ecstatic screams of my children as they expressed joy and happiness being here. Amos arrived to pick up his family in style and grace. Not only did he already have a seven-seater van, but he also rented a house in a beautiful community to ensure our welcome was royal. We all climbed into the van, buckled into our seats, then began our drive from the Seville Airport to the town of Utrera.

As the sun brightly beamed through our van and into my face, I began to go deep within my thoughts as ideas started to flow from my head. After about thirty minutes, which seemed like less than twenty, Amos's voice interrupted my daydreaming and he announced with enthusiasm and a serious calm, "Here is Utrera, guys."

We all replied with amazement and spontaneity, as we clapped with gratitude and shuffled in our seats to the music playing lightly in the background. Before the move, I remember the information I gathered about the place we decided to make our home. Utrera is a small and rural town located in the province of Sevilla, in the southern region of Spain called Andalusia, or Andalucía in Spanish. Andalusia is a very unique region surrounded by many beautiful beaches, hills, rivers, and farmland that border Spain's southern coast. Its capital is Seville, and it is populated by less than nine million people. I was happy and proud to be moving from the south of one country to the south of another, maintaining my living integrity to stay near the sun and the water. My eyes scanned outside the window as Amos slowly drove through the town. I suddenly saw this old fat man sitting on a bucket. In front of him was a small table displaying fresh seasonal fruit from what I assumed to be his farm. For a second we both just stared at each other and before I even realized, this man suddenly smiled at me; my hands quickly rose as I waved to him in excitement. His smile was genuine, and he waved back at me. I interpreted this cute old man's gesture as a beautiful yet subtle welcome to the town. I could not believe that we finally made it to Spain! Thoughts continued to flood my mind as we drove through the town and my memory flashed back to just two months prior when we initially received word and confirmation that Amos was granted the position here. I thought back on our struggles and how we overcame each obstacle with love, faith and endurance. Our children were also warriors and they battled their own wars in the past, nonetheless, they won each of them. I felt in my heart that this was our reward, and we had many more to come. I can recollect that phone call from Amos, as my mind quickly passed through memories, yet was also enjoying the extravagant architecture and landscape of Utrera's scenery. Amos called me from Georgia where he was temporarily living to obtain training for future positions while I, as explained earlier, was with the children in North Florida. My cellphone rang several times before I reached it, dashing through the dining area, dodging toys on the floor. My instinct told me it was Amos and I hated missing his calls if I didn't have to.

I answered with a playful and silly voice, "Hello, my love."

We both chuckled and before I could ask about his day, Amos bolted out, "Guess what?" with a tease.

"What?" I replied anxiously.

"I got a job offer for a position in my career field. The position is in Spain and the entire family can come!"

"What? This is an answer to our prayers!" I exclaimed as I jumped from the sofa.

My heart beat faster than my eyes could blink, and I knew God was moving pieces in our lives.

Suddenly our car stopped and so did my memories. Amos parked the van, pulled our luggage out of the back and began walking as we followed in awe. Across the way was a large and beautiful pool. Amos explained that it was our community pool and everyone in the neighborhood possessed access to it. The pool was large with an attached bar and cafeteria where adults could drink or eat while watching their children swim. We then walked a short distance to a tall, large house with a white gate. The house seemed slightly dated yet it was still attractive, elegant and much different from the homes in our country. Amos showed us around the house, and we all settled in perfectly. The children and I were very excited as well as exhausted and we were all ready to relax and eat as a family. Looking around at everyone then glancing at my husband's smile I could tell that he was relieved to have his family back with him. I knew that this experience in Spain would be amazing and I believe that the children felt it too.

August was said to be one of the hottest months in Spain and I did not see or feel any evidence of a lie. This was surely a fact seeing as how I would break out into sweats just watching my children play outside our new home. However, I enjoyed the summers most in the United States and now in Spain. The summer was the perfect season to arrive here and my children and I were already visiting the local pool almost every day until school started. My husband, sister and I were excited to construct a plan to visit islands, water parks, beaches museums and as many cities as we could think of.

The first month here in Utrera was a little tough not only on me and my children, but my husband as well. He entered his supervisory position under a boss who should have known better but lacked true leadership skills as well as respect for and from his local Spanish employees. Many workers in Spain do not take mistreatment of employees lightly. For this reason, some of Amos's team members grew frustrated with the boss and morale was very low. This led to a toxic environment in the workplace. Sporadically, during the first year, I would see my husband walk into the house with a smile of gratification to be here in Spain, yet his spirit was already being tested. Nevertheless, my husband being the professional, driven, and ambitious man he is, woke up every morning and gave it his best. Being the feisty woman that I am, I wanted to chastise his boss and those workers and explain to them how it could be a lot worse. In my short time here, I have discovered that high-performance workmanship in Spain is not as strictly enforced as it is idealized in America. Amos never complained and the children were always happy to see him come home every day, a routine we were grateful to become reacquainted with, seeing that before arriving here, Amos use to deploy many times in the military and would miss many valuable moments with us.

My interpretation of what was going on is this: Some days, Amos would sometimes have to work a five-man job by himself or with only one or two employees present. Spain has a system called "baja," an allowance for temporary incapacity. It is incomparable to any of the American unemployment and compensation programs. Essentially, if a worker was mentally, physically or psychologically injured then they could get paid time off of work, even long term. Unfortunately, this system was very easy to take advantage of in Spain, as workers could be absent from work for several months at a time with no repercussions. Although these men may or may not have been abusing this system, I believed my husband was now challenged by learning a new working system and way of life that differed greatly from that of the US. I felt that some of the workers did not know Amos yet and possibly lacked a decent relationship with the boss and past supervisor. As time progressed, the situation died down and the workers made their point as things became less hectic and strenuous for Amos. I am grateful to have a king with so much humility and pride in all he does. I think many of his coworkers began to appreciate his work ethic as well as respect his authority once they learned who Amos is and what he stood for. And he stood for respect and fairness for all.

    Living in a small town that possesses limited diversity can be uncomfortable at times. I can recall the years living in Turkey and North Dakota and feeling this similar sense of discomfort. The ill feeling was mostly from the stares. Sometimes I felt my children and I were in a clear moving box on display. Walking into the pool area many would stare. Shopping in town, many would gaze as if we were aliens. I never enjoyed this aspect of our lifestyle change, yet I could only get used to it and understand the reason. Many of these people are not exposed to diversity or change; therefore, our representation in their town amazed some, frightened others, and intrigued most. My first few months I felt alone with Amos being at work for the majority of the day and I was ready for my sister to arrive. With my Spanish underway and my stand-off type of personality, I did not foresee me making friends so soon. Nevertheless, I was positive, at peace and very happy to be in Spain. Thus, I made connections very fast and began to feel more welcomed every day. The routine of my children and I going to the pool and store each day went on for weeks until I met my first friend, Cristina Molina Gomez. Cristina worked at the local pool as a lifeguard and I would say that her love for Abi brought us together like fate.

Cristina introduced herself as Tina and that made me think of home and how it was very normal to shorten our names or give nicknames. Tina was the first person who ever extended herself to me here in Spain, and for that I will forever be grateful. When I initially met her at the pool, she explained to me how she had B2 English level certification, which is said to be the fourth level of English in Europe's common framework reference. Anyone with this level would be considered a "confident" English speaker. Tina explained this to me and politely offered her guidance should I or my children need it, and we did. She wrote down her name and number on a small piece of paper and I put it in my purse. Although it took me a few weeks to finally contact her, I did not hesitate to let her know that my family and I were interested in her offer to assist with our Spanish learning. She was very excited to oblige. She began coming to our home twice a week for one to two hours. We began lessons with me writing down simple common phrases used here in Spain and I easily memorized them. Eventually, I would find other Spanish learning avenues that worked best for me; therefore, giving Tina the opportunity to focus solely on teaching Abi. Moreover, a very beautiful friendship flourished between little Abigail and Tina. Even though Tina was in her early twenties, I felt as though Abi viewed her as a peer. Their connection was almost comical because many times when Tina attempted to give Abi a lesson, Abi would insist on playing with Tina instead. Nonetheless, over the course of a few months to a year, Tina's lessons with Abi proved to be extremely successful. Within six to eight months of Tina tutoring Abi and her mother, Tia Patri caring for our children, Abi had become practically fluent in Spanish. She even developed an "Andalusian" accent. How adorable yet correct she would sound speaking to me, her brothers or Daddy. I knew in my heart that Abi was ready for school and I was ecstatic to know that her first years of learning would begin in a different country other than the one she was born in. This same feeling applied to Aaron as well. I was always nervous about my baby boy going off to school and sometimes questioned if I should homeschool him permanently. But God knew better than I or my husband as Utrera, Spain, was the confirmation. I did not foresee Aaron attending school here in Utrera, but Amos and I had high hopes for Amari, our oldest of eight years. Amari would be attending third grade, yet I did not know exactly what school he would be attending until I met the owners of our new home. They were a nice couple and they assisted us with some things that we were still getting used to. The wife, who was a teacher herself, mentioned to me the school she was teaching at, Salesianos. She offered to show the school to me and explained that we could request a tour while inquiring about getting Amari into third grade for the upcoming school year. As we walked down the red and grey brick sidewalks, I could feel my mind drifting and being captivated by the beauty of this small town. The wife's information quickly zoned me back in as she began to explain the school system of Spain to me.

"You see, there are three different types of schools here in Spain: (1) public schools: governed and funded by the government, (2) private schools: founded, funded and governed by private sectors and or organizations, and (3) charter schools: founded and funded through private sectors and or organizations. But they also receive partial subsidized funding from the government. Some charter schools are religious while others are not."

Salesianos is considered a religious charter school. Salesianos is a magnificent school internally and externally. My only concern was exposing my Pentecostal Christian-raised children to a Catholic influence. Nevertheless, the education at this particular school was known for its prestigious atmosphere, consistent learning tactics, organization, diversity, family involvement and excellent staff. During the tour what stuck out to me most was the fact that the children at Salesianos began learning different languages at three years of age, which is the age a child is legally permitted to begin school. This was strange for me due to the fact that my baby girl, Abi, was two years of age and in America children are permitted to begin attending school at the age of four years. I was not sure how I would react to Abi going to school the very next year. As the tour came to an end and I had met most of the academic staff I felt that Salesianos was the school for my children. I was taken by surprise when I learned that this school not only possessed a third-grade slot for Amari, but they also had an open slot for Aaron's grade. My heart began to pound in anxiety yet excitement as I thought of Aaron attending school here. My fear and anxiety quickly vanished when I discussed this opportunity with Amos. His calm spirit and nonchalant personality fueled my heart with confidence, and I was happy to know that not only was Amari going to Salesianos, but my baby boy, Aaron, was going as well. Two of our children were preparing for school. Amos and I then budgeted in their uniforms, supplies, shoes and all they needed to be ready. I rapidly completed the paperwork, received the acceptance, and the bonus was there were a number of teachers that spoke English. This was common in schools in Spain. I was very pleased by the smooth process, offered help and the gratification the school displayed to have two Black American students attending their school. Not only were my boys extending the diversity of this school, but they were also native speakers of English and the academic leadership knew that my children would be an asset to them and they an asset to my children as they would quickly become fluent in Spanish.

It was September and the weather around this time in the south of Spain is amazing. Unlike in the States, school begins in September and not the end of August during the harshest heat. I can remember like it was yesterday: my two boys' first day of school in Spain at one of the best schools in this region of Spain; Colegio Salesianos Nuestra Señora del Carmen was the full name. I was both excited and nervous. I could only imagine how Amari and Aaron were feeling at this time as I skimmed through my own feelings about this day. They both woke up early that morning ready to put on their new navy blue and red uniforms accompanied with a pair of nice black dress shoes. Amos and I didn't enjoy the prices of the uniforms, but we appreciated their school culture of making it mandatory for the children to all be in proper uniform every day, even during the physical education days. I packed the boys' lunch as I became more anxious about Aaron and Amari's first day. Remembering the directions to the school we all walked together as we saw other children in their Salesianos uniforms walking as well. I was already nervous for Amari because he had been sheltered and homeschooled for most of his childhood. But I was even more on edge for Aaron.

He is so simple yet so very complex. My largest fear was that Aaron would not be able to adapt to the change of school, the routine of being around different children every day, and being apart from Mommy and Daddy. In addition, my fear for Amari was that he would be too nervous and emotional to learn due to the language barrier, that he would not make friends fast enough, or that he would not like it in general. I was wrong about both my little kings, thank God! Amari loved school and was so excited and Aaron not only adapted but evolved and flourished socially beyond my expectations.

As we walked through these excessively large double wooden and metal doors I felt as though we were in a Harry Potter movie. The school was very traditional, and the Catholic religion was displayed all throughout the design as well as the history of the school and church. We walked up the stairs and instantly we were passionately greeted by the administrative leader, José Carlos, who I quickly noticed was addressed as Don Carlos, meaning Sir Carlos. Don Carlos worked closely with the school secretary—who is equally awesome—principal, guidance counselor and school psychologist to better assist my children. He is a teacher for the special-needs children. However, he sometimes acts and helps with administrative work because of his multilingual skills. Don Carlos impressively speaks Spanish, English and French. He is a middle-aged, handsome, intelligent and charming man. He loves all of the children dearly and is very dedicated to his job, very much like most or all of the teachers and staff at Salesianos. He has been by our side since the day I toured the school, and he has not hesitated in assisting with translating. He was very patient and willing to help in any way possible. He is another Spaniard who was eager and excited to reacquaint himself with the English language and for that I was beyond grateful. Finally, we dropped our overly excited eight-year-old Amari off to his designated location, kissed him goodbye and off he ran.

Then it was Aaron's turn to be dropped off. As Amos, Don Carlos and I all walked down the wide hallway of the primary children's area, it felt as though time had slowed down and the next three minutes were all in slow motion. All of my steps down the hall felt like my feet were made of cement. I felt my heart racing as I observed what seemed to be the entire line of primary teachers standing outside their door. Staring at us in anticipation. Wondering, "Will this Negrito Americano be in my class?" We seemed to have passed about four to five classrooms feeling like time was still slowing down. Catching the eyes of each teacher I could observe they were all attractive, nicely dressed and shared my uncertainty of who would be the teacher of my son Aaron? As we reached toward the end of the hallway, my eyes fell on a teacher. She was young, petite and had a slightly slouched posture. Her spirit seemed extremely calm yet confident. Our eyes met and my spirit was slowly put at ease. As the feeling of ease came over me, time began to catch back up to reality and I could hear Don Carlos introducing us to Aaron's new teacher, Celia Revarro Gutiérrez. Her slight smile was forced yet comforting. It seemed as though she had been previously briefed on Aaron's conditions and was ready to accept the challenge. You see, Aaron was diagnosed with level 1 autism back in America but here in Spain he is considered essentially normal. Nevertheless, the fact is that Aaron is different, yet he is also unique, resilient, strong and ambitious. He smiled at Celia and she smiled at him. He walked into the classroom ready to embark on his new journey of school. As time passed and Aaron integrated nicely into the routine of attending school, I would credit 40 percent of his progress to his teacher Celia. I look forward to seeing how my babies all succeed the next year, but I can proudly say that this year I am greatly enjoying watching my children develop their personalities, find their talents and discover the world here in Spain. I could not have imagined a greater experience for them especially my firstborn, Amari. I can candidly proclaim that at times I find myself imagining I am an eight-year-old girl living in Spain, questioning how the experience would be for me and how I would feel living this life. Amari is very intelligent, fun, funny and always has been a happy child. A load was lifted off my shoulders when I heard about his first day at Salesianos. He spoke about the many friends he made and how he adored his main teacher, Don Manuel. Amari gave us much insight into his new teacher and his many awesome classmates. When I first met Don Manuel, I remember thinking he was very young and displayed much enthusiasm. Amari bragged that he had the best teacher in the school, that Don Manuel was fun, stylish, intelligent, charismatic, and absolutely an awesome teacher. As the year evolved, I came to love Amari's teacher myself. I observed that his English was limited but I could tell that he understood English better than he could speak it, which helped us communicate better than with the other teachers. I loved Don Manuel's young swag. He has a beautiful wife, and she was six months pregnant when Amari started school, and now that pregnancy is a healthy little boy who is now two years old. Amazing how time flies! Don Manuel was the absolute perfect first teacher for Amari because he was both kind and patient with him. He loved music and dancing and was an expert on social media, which were all things Amari admired about his teacher. He even has a YouTube channel in which he helps teach and explain some of his schoolwork; that was extremely helpful for us all, not just for Amari and his classmates. Amari and Aaron were flourishing in school and that gave tremendous confirmation to Amos and me that we made the right choice for our family.

Not only did this work out perfectly for my family, however; Zipporah and D'iona were embarking on this journey with us as well. Zipporah is my older sister of one year and I could tell many people assumed she was younger than me, based on our life dynamics. Zipporah is a well-known poetess throughout our home state of Florida. She is a licensed cosmetologist and veteran like myself and Amos. Her skin has the dark brown beautiful tone of ripe cocoa. She is a people person, party animal, and spiritual being all rolled into one petite, muscular-toned body. She is a lover of women and not ashamed to express it. Her unique beauty and presence turn heads and demands attention. When she walks into the room, she is the life of the party. All of these were perfect qualities to be able to integrate into a culture such as Spain. I enjoyed my sister accompanying me wherever I would go because she was sort of my "icebreaker." I was proud to have a cool, strong and beautiful big sister that is always there for me when I need her. Zipporah is a single woman with no children; therefore, she played the role of the "cool auntie" for the children and they all treasured her presence here. She has always been a free spirit and I believed this venture to Spain was something she needed and wanted. I can remember our many conversations about leaving America and trying something different. I did not raise my hopes to the idea of her coming to Spain when I first mentioned the move to Zipporah because I did not want to be disappointed if she changed her mind. Something very common of Zipporah. But she sold most of her things, packed her and D'iona's lives up in just eight boxes, shipped them to our address and they were in route.

I was so psyched about picking my sister and niece up from the Seville Airport the day they arrived. It was a cool yet sunny afternoon when Amos, I and the children left to go retrieve them. I imagined hugging them tightly and I felt like a child thinking of all the new things I wanted to introduce them to. Not only was I overjoyed about my new life and sharing it with my two best friends, Amos and my sister, but I was also very grateful that Zipporah was bringing D'iona along. D'iona was ten years of age when they first arrived in Spain. She is very timid around most people until she feels comfortable. She is observant, wise, sweet, very sensitive, and loving. She was extremely fired up and grateful to be in Spain with us, but the absence of her mother, Keturah, placed a void in D'iona's heart that we simply could not fill. For that reason, D'iona's happiness and appreciation were limited. Nonetheless, Zipporah and I were optimistic and ready to be her emotional support. D'iona required more attention and we felt she could learn a lot through this experience not only in Spain, but in our family of three smaller children than herself. D'iona was the oldest child now and this gave her more responsibility, a sense of family unity and time with a man she could not only call Uncle but view as a father. She became my little helper and like my own daughter during the summer prior to this move; therefore, I knew in my heart we would all continue to mesh well, and her healing would begin here with us.

As we all pulled up to the house, I could hear the excitement in D'iona's voice as she and Amari ranted on about their future in Spain. The children were happy to show Auntie Zipporah and Cousin DD their new home. At the house I made the space comfortable and cozy for Zipporah and D'iona and I was happy to show them both. The house was a three-bedroom, two-bathroom home; therefore, Zipporah stayed in the third bedroom, D'iona stayed in the room with the two boys, and Abi with Amos and me. We were all comfortable and this was only temporary. Zipporah's plan was to find a place of her own and I was happy to help. Until then, we all stayed as a tribe together.

Each day consisted of us dropping the children off to school, eating breakfast with the ladies then exploring the town. I believe the first few months were a little difficult for Zipporah to get used to, seeing that this town lacked diversity. But I reassured her that we are the diversity and there are other ethnicities here from the airbase, Africa and many other surrounding countries. The same day that Zipporah arrived my point made was proven. That evening after school, Zipporah and I were walking to a park with the children, my friend Vanessa and her children. On our journey we met a beautiful African mother named Fatou. When we saw Fatou, our spirits instantly connected and we both knew she would be a new friend. Fatou was a beautiful Nubian queen from Senegal. She was so cool, and we have so much in common. I was very impressed because she was fluent in four languages including French, English, Spanish and her native tongue, which is "Wolof." She had two beautiful young children and they both spoke Spanish, English and French as well. Adama, her son and youngest child was adorable. His eyes were piercing, and his face was like a perfect brown baby doll. He was very timid at first but once he became comfortable, he was more relaxed, sweet and playful. He and Abi played well whenever we would link. As I, Zipporah, Vanessa and Fatou socialized, my attention slowly was redirected to a quick interaction between Amari and Fatou's daughter and oldest child, Fama. This little dark brown girl was beautiful, intelligent and very energetic. She was fearless, and I loved how multilingual she is. She is a great soccer player and loved to dance like Amari. As I redirected my attention to the children, I noticed my eight-year-old approach Fama. I could tell Amari was happy to meet another melanated child like himself and was anxious to talk and play with her.

"*Tu nombre es*?" Amari asked.

"Fama," she answered.

Amari then gestured for them to play together, and to my surprise Fama obliged. They both ran off to the park and all I could feel was pride. My son was picking up Spanish very fast and he displayed confidence in speaking, something I lacked when I was his age. I was surprised and proud of Amari. He saw a brown child like himself but still approached her in Spanish, as to not assume she did not speak the native tongue of Spain, which is common for many people to do. "How intelligent," I thought aloud.

As I ventured back to the conversation between us women, I could remember Fatou explaining that her husband Samba would be arriving home soon from a job he encountered in another country. Work was not easy to find in the south of Spain for natives, let alone non-natives. However, for the natives and non-natives who did find work, they often struggled with finding a position close to home. Some would be forced to commute 50 miles or more each day. It was common in these small towns for the mothers to stay home with the children as the fathers worked. Because of the lack of employment in the south, many people were forced to commute to other towns, cities or even countries to find income. This was something Fatou and her husband battled with. Nevertheless, I knew in my heart that this would change for their family. Despite the negative ideas many Spaniards possessed toward the African natives, my family and I knew that many lacked knowledge of not just them but of us, Black Americans as well. We as humans want to evolve, and we strive for a good life. Sometimes that life is in a country other than our own. Nevertheless, I think that Fatou's family adjusted to Spain as best as they could.

I can remember later on into the months of being here when we all first met Samba, her husband. Because of his job being out of the country we met him over the phone. He was kindred in spirit with his wife, Fatou. He is handsome, kind, intelligent and always willing to help. When he finally arrived back home with his family, we all invited them over so that the husbands could meet. Our families all blended well, and everyone enjoyed the time spent. There were other times when he and Fama would come by our house in the evening so that Samba could pick Amari up. Both he and Fama were helping Amari improve his soccer skills. Amari appreciated this time and was happy to learn the skill of soccer, a common sport called *futbol* here all throughout Spain. Samba played on a professional team in his past and was a perfect teacher for his daughter and Amari. This unity between our family and theirs gave us all a sense of unity and pride.

It was the second day that Zipporah and D'iona had arrived and Zipporah was ready to explore the nightlife here in Utrera. We decided to attend a local beer festival held every year in the month of October for the entire weekend. We asked Tina's mother, Tia Patri to watch the children that night while we attended the beer fest. Everything was within walking distance so we walked to the location, which was "La Plaza de Toros," a common area where Utrera would host many of their main events.

It was a humid yet cool October night. I could see Zipporah taking in every moment as I had been doing since the moment that we arrived in Spain. La Plaza de Toros was in the direction toward the Parque de Consolación (Consolation Park), so we walked the paseo while watching the night stars. When we arrived, the right side of the stadium was lined with tents, tables with benches and many people. Everyone seemed to be enjoying themselves while with their families. There were children running around playing, men and women talking and laughing. To the left side, there was a huge bar full of various types of European beers to choose from. My husband, sister and I all had a great time for we enjoy beer and were happy to try new ones. We talked, laughed and danced. There was a particular song called "No M'Arrecojo (50 Años En Familia)" by Diego Carrasco that was playing, and it seemed to have touched our souls. Although it was a flamenco Spanish song and we did not understand the lyrics. However, the African rhythm and origin of the song seemed to be our universal translator. As I watched and recorded my sister and husband dancing to this beautiful song, I noticed in the corner of my eye the many people watching and enjoying the view of us enjoying their culture and town. Some people even retrieved their phones and begin to record themselves. It was sort of strange yet comical. We continued the night with beer, freshly grilled chicken and snacks. This was a night to remember and the beginning of our many nightlife adventures to come.

As I take a deep breath and look around, I notice my huge life change. What a beautiful life we created, and my fulfillment has been more than I could conceptualize. So many doors have opened, and opportunities arrived. For example, not only am I getting the chance to live abroad outside of the military with my husband and children, but my sister and niece are here as well. With God's help, I have conquered many battles and my path is now clear for me to soar. One of my top goals was to lose weight and sustain a healthier diet. This I knew would be possible and feasible because I lived in a town where walking is the main transportation, and my workout junkie sister was here. We started dancing on my house terrace and I can remember the feeling of sweating and burning calories under the sun, doing something that not only I love but the children love as well. We would pump up our gospel, afro beats, or reggaeton and move to its rhythm as a fun workout. This started as a silly and funny vibe my sister and I had, but soon became a class. Let me elaborate. My sister, being the outgoing and fun type would often find a reason to dance and she did not care who was around. Some of the mothers at breakfast soon became not only my friends but also members of a workout dance class my sister and I kicked off. I can think back to the time when the subject was mentioned as we all giggled about it. Not knowing that these words soon became reality. Many of the mothers we socialized with and had breakfast with loved to dance as well and I assume they were looking for an outlet and a way to connect with us. We first began dancing at local parks and meeting wherever we could. We made videos, laughed and sweated drops of joy. I had never done anything like this and the thrill of it growing forced me to brainstorm.

"Sis, we should find a place and start a dance class," I suggested with enthusiasm to Zipporah. This idea entered my head out of empathy for myself and many mothers like me. We are often overwhelmed with our children's needs and sometimes the needs of our husbands that we forget about our own. I would have conversations about this often with these strong and brave women and friends from back home. I not only needed this workout class, but I wanted to share the jollification with the other mothers. I thought it best for Zipporah to teach the class as I would run the warm-ups. This felt divine and I was ready to indulge. We asked our brother's art studio, NRashadstudios, to create our logo. We took our logo and made flyers at one of the mother's, Teresa's, printing shop and quickly began advertising. Another mother Conso A. asked her friend who owned a gym, if we could make an agreement to use his large exercise room two days a week. He acceded and the "Hermanas Bailando" class was launched.

A few weeks later and I was sitting quietly on the red rubber covered gym floor, dripping with sweat as I was proud of both my sister and myself. We turned our dream into a reality. Additionally, I was proud of myself for shedding so much excess weight that I've wanted to lose for years! Not to mention that both my athletic and dancing abilities have significantly improved. When I arrived in Spain, I became different. My eating habits, cravings, and so on were diluted. I began to eat less meat replacing it with fruit and vegetables ensuring my energy is not lowered when dealing with the children. We walked to most places because Amos had to use our only vehicle for work. I was and still remain very happy with our lives here in Spain. In my eyes, my peace and happiness were 60 percent of my weight loss. When I arrived in Spain, I weighed about 170 pounds. Eight months later, I weighed only 135 pounds. I had lost approximately 35 pounds in just eight months!

But after Zipporah arrived, my weight loss seemed to accelerate as Zipporah and I are here in this dance workout class twice a week every Monday and Thursday from three thirty to four thirty! The gym owner, Jesús, happily welcomed us every week. Thinking back on the day I first met Jesús, I was not sure if he would agree due to his serious gestures and nonchalant yet conceited attitude. But I also could only understand about 45 percent of what he was saying. Overall, in my observation, Jesús a is serious, well-disciplined, fit, intelligent and respectful businessman. I believe he saw this class as an opportunity, potential profit and exposure. When he made his demands and we all agreed, we all faithfully attended the class, and it was fun and helpful. Zipporah being the energetic one would always have us all lain out on the floor wobbling in our knees to catch our breaths. We all enjoyed her being our instructor, but she is also a single woman who traveled often. One of my obstacles I overcame during my first year here in Spain was going against many of my own odds and facing my fears I only created. For instance, I reluctantly and nervously led the dance class when Zipporah went on vacation for the holidays. I was not sure how I would lead this class compared to Zipporah leading it daily, yet as my doubt crept in the words of Zipporah rang through my head. "You can do anything if you set your mind to it."

I smiled with confidence and also thought of Conso A's encouragement and excitement to keep the classes going. We had a total of ten faithful members. However, during the holidays only three members attended the classes. This did not discourage or offend me, but it relieved me. Not only was I happy and motivated to have fun and keep us in good shape, but the member count gave me comfort. All of the women remained pumped and I was proud to have defeated that vacillation. In short, every member, old and new, relished the dance class and our names were being mentioned all around town. I know that many of the mothers appreciated this time spent and looked forward to it continuing.

Not only were we all enjoying the new endeavors of Spain, but we were also making great progress. Zipporah, Amos and I have achieved so much as a tribe and our togetherness has helped us all succeed in a new country. It can be difficult to survive without connections and many of those we have successfully established. During our first year we all made great connections with many of the mothers and their families. We also made a few connections with people from the airbase. I am full of gratefulness when I see the joy in my children; when I feel the joy within myself and I acknowledge the joy in my husband and entire family. I would admit that I feared for only one of my children as stated before; that fear was geared toward Aaron. With his unique habits and obsessive behavior, I feared for his development here in Spain. But that fear slowly vanished as each day introduced him to new ideas and authentic situations. I especially relished his improvement in communication. I would have never known that placing Aaron in an environment that may not be comfortable to him at first was the answer to tearing down many of his walls psychologically, and mine mentally. Not only was he making progress, but he was making friends.

It was the first week of December when Aaron attended his first classmate birthday party. Many of the parties were held after school on Fridays at a private venue. It was the birthday of little Martina who was as cute as a button. She wore light pink glasses and was as sweet and smart as she could be! She reminded me of a female version of the little boy from the movie *Stuart Little*. When we arrived, all of the parents were very friendly and welcoming. The mother of Martina is Ángeles and I was able to meet her husband, Antonio Sanchez. He was very nice, and he spoke English fairly well. We talked for a bit and I found out his job was similar to my husband's. They both worked on the airbase. Antonio mentioned to me that he would see my husband around the base and he just knew that he was the father of Aaron. He made me laugh so hard when he tried to imitate the way Southern Americans speak. It was nice meeting more parents and Aaron had a great time, which made me extremely happy.

Happiness was a common feeling I encounter constantly while living in Spain. I was always finding out new history about this country through the new friends I had made. They enjoyed sharing with me the pride in their culture and I enjoyed sharing mine with them. For instance, their Spanish Constitution Day (Día de la Constitución Española) is December 6. Essentially, 1977 was the year Spain broke away from being a dictatorship country. On this day at many schools the children would bring red and yellow balloons, representing the colors of the Spanish flag. To many legends and historians, the flag was a symbol of bullfighting. The red represents the blood spill of the bull while the yellow represents the sand of the arena where the blood would fall. Learning about this particular tradition was hard for me to swallow because I believe in only taking the lives of animals for the use of survival and not fun or play. I would respectfully listen and show honor toward each person for educating me. They were happy and proud to explain it all to me and I was appreciative. It seemed as though I was making connections every week. Everyone wanted the privilege of meeting my family and me, whether it was for a coffee or for a family event. I tried to attend each invite, but I could not. Nevertheless, the many invitations made me feel welcomed. My children took part in most birthday parties they were invited to and my husband and I made an effort to unite with many of the Spaniards in town, more than Americans on base. We knew that integrating ourselves would not only increase our Spanish intake, but it would also give us the full experience of the country.

It was the second week of December and we had already been summoned to many events. This particular event we attended was actually a BBQ. This made me think of home and the many family BBQs my parents would host in South Florida. However, this was a little different than home. This was an Andalusian-style BBQ. It was not just a small typical backyard BBQ with family and a few friends. Here in Spain your friends are your family and many of the children in school grow up together like siblings, which I believe to be a beautiful way to evolve from child to adult. I would imagine my children experiencing those same connections while here in this quaint town.

Pulling up to the location of the BBQ, I noticed that this was a large country home, elegantly decorated, yet rurally comfortable and natural. The hostess, Cristina, a mother of one of Aaron's classmates invited my family and me. I could not resist her request for us to attend, so I consented our attendance and there we were. As we entered the area, we heard loud music, laughter, and glasses clinking. A large crowd of many friends and family, older and younger, greeted us with traditional kisses. Due to Amos's work schedule, we arrived a few hours after the time it began yet it was not even noticed or shamed; it was simply understood. By the time we arrived all of the people were feeling great. Everyone began to speak to us one by one, all trying to speak their best English. Amos would step away from time to time as the fathers would pull him into conversation. Some of the men at this BBQ displayed cooking expertise, which enticed my husband. Amos is my favorite chef and not just because he is my husband and I support him, yet the professionalism and perfectionism aspects of his cooking places his flavors on a chart I never knew existed. I could see the competitive side come out at times when others would speak of their skills and/or challenge his. This tickled me as I watched this very thing happen right before my eyes at this BBQ. The beauty and friendly competition are always fun to watch, nonetheless, I could see that Amos was also learning and that was something he always welcomed. This BBQ was an event Cristina and her husband Antonio Serrano hosted each year during the winter at his family country-side house. Many different people would attend this BBQ every year and I could see on both their faces that Cristina and Antonio were proud to have everyone in their home and in their presence. Sharing food, drinks, conversations and love. I can remember mentioning D'iona's vegetarian diet to Cristina the day prior and she was ready to serve graciously. She began to disappear and reappear in and out of the house. Each time her hands were full of vegetarian dishes. She served D'iona like she was a princess and that meant so much to us. We ate freshly grilled pig skin, various pork, beef, and chicken dishes, pasties, snacks and much more. Each dish was different and unique. Some had great flavor, and some did not. I was still getting used to the difference of foods here compared to my country. However, I do appreciate the naturalness in the foods and water here in Europe. Spain, being known for its great agriculture, was full of fresh markets. Some cities possessed them on every street. Eating some of these dishes at this BBQ confirmed this observation. These dishes had fresh ingredients, and many were homemade. In less than an hour I was full of beer and great food. Cristina's husband, Antonio Serrano, came and introduced himself to us as we ate and socialized with others. Antonio is a well-known veterinarian here in Utrera. He and I clicked because of our common love for horses. He and Cristina have two beautiful children. Little Antonio was four, Aaron's age, and their daughter, Blanca, was three. Antonio is charming, smart and kind. He spoke a little English and I could tell that he enjoyed it. I could also observe that he was a great father by the way he served D'iona along with his wife.

Speaking English made it easy to stand out and become noticed. To my surprise there was another family associated with the airbase at this BBQ. A Cuban American man Jorge and his Japanese wife, Aika, and their three small children. I could tell they were both happy to hear American English and to meet another family from home. Jorge and Aika are the parents of another one of Aaron's classmates, Luna. She was an adorable mix of Jorge and Aika. She spoke a little Spanish, Japanese and of course English. She and Aaron played great together, and she seemed to understand Aaron's solitude. They also have a beautiful eight-year-old daughter, Susie, and three-year-old son, Robert. Jorge is active-duty US military, and he is also from my hometown of Miami, Florida. In my personal opinion, Jorge is a bit pretentious. But once I looked past his flaws, I noticed that he is really a cool person. His wife, Aika, was the exact opposite of her husband. She was very timid, sweet and humble. She did not say much, and she would always smile. She seemed to be greatly involved with the events of school and as time progressed, I realized that this was common. To be immersed in the activities of school. I loved meeting these new families and building more connections. As conversations continued and food was passed around all night, we could not help but wonder who was grilling this meat to such perfection. We soon received the answer to our question. A kind man with an apron on appeared from the back with a plate of freshly grilled beef. I could see the juice leaking from the meat and smell the smoke drifting from the plate. As we all indulged and ate the meat off of every bone, our mouths began to water and taste buds danced. Amos and I were so impressed and were esteemed to meet Alexander. "The French Cook" I began to call him. I think he was flattered as he smiled and laughed in response to my nickname for him. Alexander is the husband of María José and father of little Alexandra. Little Alexandra is another one of Aaron's classmates. Time passed as we all enjoyed one another's company, eating everything served before us. The French cook was a husky, handsome man with a full beard on his face. He then reappeared out of the night with two fresh chickens on each shoulder. I could tell that my husband and I were both asking ourselves the same question.

"How is he going to barbecue two whole chickens within this short time frame?" I muttered to Amos. He smiled in response and shrugged his shoulders. Well, to our astonishment two hours later he began serving everyone the juiciest, most tender and flavorful grilled chicken that I've ever tasted. He sliced the chicken into thick pieces and laid them on freshly baked Spanish bread. His dish presentation was superb and his spirit to serve was even better. Amos chuckled as we enjoyed the dish and admitted to Alexander what we were thinking. We all laughed at the many ideas that came through our heads of Alexander accomplishing what had seemed like an impossible task.

Amos and I enjoyed talking to Alexander. His passion for cooking was both intoxicating and admirable. His philosophy on life appeared to be centered around cooking, servitude, and most importantly family. He expressed that he loves to cook because he relishes the idea of sharing and providing. His mother is French, and he was born and raised in France. But his father is from Spain; therefore, he speaks French, Spanish and English, which is also impressive. Although Alexander was living in Spain with a Spanish wife, he seemed to identify more with his French heritage. Every person I spoke to was interesting and excited to share with me their story. I met so many mothers and fathers, friends and lovers, sisters and brothers. I also met Javier, the husband of Anita and father of twins, Xavier and Martina. Both Javier and Anita are active-duty Spanish military members and they seemed perfect for one another. Javier is handsome, vibrant, intelligent and easy to talk to. He also speaks a little English as did many of the attendees of this party. Both Anita and Javi were always willing to assist me with my Spanish, and I did not hesitate to take advantage of that help. I would jot down notes as they would correct or inject me with knowledge of the language. We all linked perfectly that night.

I watched as Abi became attached to Aika because of her calm spirit, listened as Jorge expressed gratitude to meet us, and felt delight as I saw Antonio Sanchez pull D'iona from her shy shell by engaging her with a question.

"Are you learning any Spanish, D'iona?" he asked in English.

"A little," she responded in English.

D'iona and I were sitting on the sofa when Antonio Sanchez leaned on the arm of the sofa, making direct eye contact with D'iona. He began to explain to D'iona that it's imperative that she put forth all of her effort in learning Spanish because living in another country is a rare opportunity and she should seize the moment. I'm not sure what led Antonio Sanchez to speak this truth and give DD this advice, but he was absolutely correct! I was very appreciative that he took time to explain that to my niece for it was almost as if the spirit of God spoke through him. I was surprised to hear Aika's observation as she mentioned how comfortable I seemed when exchanging affection with Spaniards. I never saw myself as an affectionate woman but living here has obviously altered that in me. On the other hand, I suppose that I am used to this way of greeting because the southern Spanish ways are very similar to Southern American ways. Friendly, affectionate and welcoming, yet nosy and cautious at the same time.

Toward the end of the night, everyone was feeling tipsy and enjoying multiple conversations. Meanwhile, as the night wrapped up Antonio Serrano informed me that he, Amos and Alexander had decided to have a cook-off. This amused Amos and it caused me to look at the wife of Alexander, María José, in fascination. She was so sweet, beautiful and petite. I wanted to ask her a question but was not sure how to say it in Spanish, so I used my Spanish translator. I handed María José my phone with the question. She took the phone, read the message, and burst into laughter. She then showed the message to her husband and everyone around her. They all together died of laughter! I was slightly confused because to me, it was a legitimate question, yet I was also amused to see them all tickled by my honest curiosity.

¡Tu marido es tan buen cocinero! ¿Como estas tan delgada? Translation: "Your husband is such a great cook! How are you so thin?"

"Gracias," María José responded, once she found the breath to speak.

"That's a good one!" Alexander exclaimed as he continued to chuckle.

A few more hours passed, and the party was ending. Most of the children, including mine, were asleep and ready to go home. We packed the children in the car, grabbed our bags and food, said our goodbyes and headed home. After changing the children and everyone was settled, I took a break to sit under the stars and thank God for all of our amazing experiences.

Sometimes I would sit out in the night's peace and quiet for hours. I can remember my first time here in Utrera, Spain, sitting under the stars in solitude. This became a daily reflection for me, and I was grateful I could have this time to steal away for a moment. I assumed my neighbors would hear my music sometimes or smell my fresh herbs burning. But neither neighbor on my right or left ever mentioned anything to me. They all seemed to be kind and to themselves. The first time that I met my neighbor to the right named Ms. Conso was on our terrace one morning shortly after Zipporah arrived. We all loved the terrace and we would spend a lot of time there. This was our favorite spot to play our jams, dance, have a drink, and so on. The air was always fresh, and the sun was warm in the cool breeze. One morning I came up to the terrace to find my sister comfortably struggling to communicate with our neighbor. It was sort of funny. Walking toward them in amusement I attempted to assist my sister. Ms. Conso and I politely introduced ourselves and I used the small amount of Spanish I possessed to explain our living arrangements. I exclaimed to Ms. Conso that Zipporah was living with us temporarily and that she was looking to find her own home. I could tell she did not understand fully, but she got the importance of what I was trying to convey. Ms. Conso then asked me a common question that I was asked often.

"How long will you all be living here in Spain?"

Ms. Conso asked with her arms leaning onto the wall. She already appeared comfortable around my sister and me and that made me relaxed as well. Thinking about her question, I did not hesitate to give her an answer, for it was the same as I have given to others.

"I don't know but I think for a long time," I replied with faith and surety.

My mind ventured to the future for a moment and I could see my children older, fluently speaking to their friends in Spanish; I saw Amos preparing each day to open his restaurant in the evenings and managing the children's music skills during the day, but most importantly I saw myself publishing this very book.

My next interaction with Ms. Conso was also on the terrace. It was during the time her daughter was there for a visit. Ms. Conso's daughter lives in Utrera and visits her parents often. Aaron was on the terrace with me when he and Ms. Conso first met. She instantly fell in love with him and showered him with love. Without Ms. Conso asking I openly explained to her in

Spanish that Aaron was on the autism spectrum. She was very surprised because in her eyes, he behaved normally. He could speak, dress himself and use the restroom on his own. Aaron counted to ten for them in Spanish and it was remarkably adorable. Ms. Conso then lifted Aaron up, brought him over to her side of the terrace, and proceeded to interact with him by playing hand games and running around. She then went into her outside storage closet to find a toy for him. She had done the same for Abi in the past because she fell in love with Abi as well.

Then there was another if only quick interaction we encountered with Ms. Conso that was a bit comical to me. Zipporah and I were having our usual morning session. Ms. Conso came out in her cute little pink house robe. We greeted each other; she asked a few questions about our ages. Ms. Conso was surprised to find out that Zipporah was older than me, that she was single with no children.

"*Eres una soltera?*" Ms. Conso asked with a smirk on her face.

Zipporah and I laughed abruptly at her response because she displayed a jester of "to each his own" on her face. She then said her exit greeting and left. I enjoyed these moments with my neighbor Ms. Conso because she was a genuine and honest person. She was kind yet stern, sweet yet feisty. I knew that every encounter with her would be a pleasure. For example, there was another time in the afternoon when my children and I were on the terrace dancing to music. Ms. Conso reacquainted herself with Aaron, watched as we danced and stayed to talk with us for a while. She even fussed at Amari for unsafely sitting on the top wall. I was slightly embarrassed as the mother that I hadn't noticed myself. However, I was appreciative that she was comfortable and concerned enough to correct him. I noticed that this is a common behavior of all mothers. We are all mothers to all children. She then took Aaron into her home once again in search of a gift for him. All she could find was an old Papa Noel (Santa Claus). The toy was Papa Noel on the top of a unicycle with brass cymbals in his hands. When turned on, the unicycle spins while Papa Noel clashes the cymbals in his hands. Unfortunately, the toy had no batteries. But Ms. Conso didn't give up that easy! She quickly rushed down her stairs in search of batteries for the toy. She emerged five minutes later with the correct size batteries. Aaron was a little nervous or frightened with the toy at first. But I don't suspect that Ms. Conso noticed. She placed the batteries into the toy and proceeded to turn it on, but the toy would not move. Suddenly with eagerness Aaron took Papa Noel and sat at the table. We all continued to dance while Ms. Conso happily spectated. She was impressed with Amari's dance moves and Abi's rhythm. A funny observation was that Abi had a tight hold of Ms. Conso's two fingers the entire time that she danced and did not let go.

All of a sudden, Ms. Conso shouted, "Mira!" We looked at her as she pointed toward Aaron at the table with delight and surprise in her eyes. The toy was working! Aaron fixed the toy, and no one knew how. It was a mystery to us all and we were in admiration and exhilaration at the sight of this toy now working. After my first interaction with Ms. Conso, I began to see her more often. I could observe that she has a great sense of style and that she is a great mother. I was happy to have a great neighbor who loved my children and respected my lifestyle and my culture. Ms. Conso is kind, very brash, fun and wise. The children and I like her a lot.

One evening in mid-December I saw Ms. Conso again while having my morning meditation. We exchanged pleasantries and she asked me about the children. She asked how the boys were doing in school and about their day. I told her on this particular day both boys had excursions. In Spain they call field trips excursions. She then asked what I was writing as she glanced at the small green journal in my right hand. I explained how I love to write in my free time. I then elaborated to her on my upcoming book and that I was writing down all my beautiful experiences here in Spain; that in one year I would publish a book about it all. She was surprised and happy to have heard this information. Her response gave me so much life! She asked me if the book would be in Spanish, suggesting that she would be honored to read it. I assured Ms. Conso that the book would be definitely published in English and Spanish. This made her smile and view me differently. She then told me that she wanted a copy.

"*Claro, claro,* of course" I expressed with a promise.

We exchanged a few more words that morning, she politely greeted me goodbye and firmly patted me on my shoulders.

"*Luego,*" Ms. Conso whispered.

"See you later," I responded in Spanish with a bright smile on my face. This exchange between Ms. Conso and I really encourage me. It made me feel good to know that the local people were interested to see how I view their country and culture as a Black American. Without even realizing it, Ms. Conso, my first neighbor in Utrera made my day.

It was easy to make acquaintances with the people in my neighborhood because many people love spending time outdoors. I recognize that many people enjoy lunch and dinner outside in the cool breeze. They all would eat and dine together as a family and that was always a refreshing sight to see. Not only did we routinely see our neighbor Ms. Conso, but we often saw our young neighbor Diego on the left. I first met him after Zipporah, and I had to ring his doorbell to see if they knew whose car was parked in our parking spot. We repeated the same scenario with Diego a few times. Sometimes his mother would park in our spot for a short period, which caused a little tension. Nevertheless, the issue would often be resolved in peace as we graciously asked them to refrain from invading our spot. Diego is the son of the owner of the house. His mother is a French-born woman who is now a registered nurse here in Spain. He also has a younger teenage sister, and she is nice as well. Diego's English is decent, which is what connected us as neighbors. We would briefly exchange words in English from time to time and I respected his effort. Diego and his friends all were young and vibrant. They seemed to have a gathering every night with friends in their front yard. They were never too rowdy or disrespectful. He expressed to me how he attends college in Seville, that he was taking courses in English. Although I just met him, I was actually proud of young Diego for expanding his education. One day, while D'iona and I were on the terrace dancing, Diego came out to hang out his clothes to dry. He quietly spectated as I danced.

Then he submitted: "I can dance too, you know."

I instantly stopped dancing and turned to Diego in surprise.

"What you got?" I responded in enthusiasm, challenging his words.

Diego then put his music on the speaker and proceeded to dance. His moves were authentic, and he had swag in his rhythm. He was a good dancer, and I was impressed. Diego is young, kind, intelligent, and friendly. His friends all seemed nice and respectful as well. My sister and I would hear him and his friends freestyling to their music and in my opinion they sounded decent. They were all good rappers in my eyes and they always seemed to be having fun and enjoying one another, not out finding trouble.

In just a few short months my life went from stay-at-home mother without seeing my husband every day in America to living in Spain with my whole family together again. I was full of exaltation as I got dressed one evening for yet another invite thinking upon this subject of happiness. Christmas was quickly approaching, and I could recall feeling slight moments of apprehension as I mistakenly made plans to attend multiple holiday functions. Nevertheless, this was my first year in this country and I wanted to take advantage of the opportunities to experience the culture as much as I could. The dance class my sister and I started led us to that opportunity. Sliding my dress over my now fit body as I pulled up my locs(hair). I glanced at the clock and realized I was running late for the gym's holiday dinner. As in the United States it was traditional for companies, groups, bars, gyms and families throughout the many towns and cities of Spain to host a big holiday dinner. Each person would pay a flat rate for the dinner to one person and arrangements would be made. Zipporah, Chelle, Amos and I decided that we would attend the gym's dinner because we wanted to show rapport. We were appreciative to Jesús for allowing us to utilize his space for our fitness dance class. We also saw this as a unique situation to have fun while getting to know others who attend and/or manage the gym. Because Zipporah was running late to pick up Chelle, we were all running late. Chelle was one of Zipporah's closest friends from Florida. She came to visit for a few months, and we were happy to welcome her to Spain. When we arrived, Jesús, the owner of the Coliseum Gym in Utrera was at the head of the table accompanied by some familiar faces and others we did not know. Everyone was dressed to impressed, looking amazing. This year it was located at a beautiful and elegant restaurant called El Bouquet Tapas in Utrera. The lunch started at two thirty but we of course had to be fashionably late. Not to mention that Spaniards are equally not punctual people. By this time Zipporah and I had been doing our dance class for over a month and had developed close bonds, friendships and work relationships. Isabel, Tina's younger sister, was already there with a friend and had messaged me numerous times asking me where we were. When we finally arrived, I asked Isabel to meet us outside and she did. She looked absolutely stunning in her velvet black dress, short in length but with long sleeves. She had on sheer stockings with black heels. Isabel met us outside and proudly escorted us inside. I thought we would be sitting inside the café of the restaurant, but she kept walking into a narrow hallway that led into a huge, closed room full of beautifully designed tables. All of the tables were filled with beautiful men and women dressed nicely. As we walked into the room reflecting our melanin and energy with hellos and big smiles, I began to feel the stares of admiration. I was in a sexy blue and gray sparkle dress and Amos was in a nice dress shirt with a flower design and nicely fitted khakis. Both Zipporah and Chelle had on beautiful black dresses and classy red coats. We all greeted everyone and sat to dine. We arrived after drinks and refreshments were served yet just in time for the five-course meal. The servers began to bring out platters of meats, fish, rice, pastas and salads. This dinner was different than at home due to the fact that we ate all the dishes together. I would grab some rice from the left side and serve myself with beef or fish nuggets on the right. I liked this style of eating because it made everything equal between us all. After stuffing our faces and socializing for a few hours we began to wrap the afternoon up and get into the night. Our group left the restaurant around half past seven and walked around town for about thirty minutes while taking pictures. We ended up at the Minibar, which was packed from wall to wall. Minibar was a very popular bar in Utrera, and its name suited its appearance. It was small on the inside yet could hold a large group on the outside. The air was extremely cold, but the massive group of people warmed up the space. We all ordered up a few drinks, laughed and talked. I ended up running into Conso A., one of the mothers I became close with at Salesianos. Conso A. was there with her cousins. It seemed more like a family reunion for her. She was very excited to introduce me to her cousins. Most of her company were a little hesitant and/or timid but I had become acquainted with that reaction while here in this small town. I politely greeted them all, made small talk with the little Spanish

I knew, and everyone began to loosen up. We all laughed and drank as we became more and more tipsy.

There was a moment at Minibar behind the plaza when I was standing alone. Hundreds of people scattered through the entire alley full of small bars. The sound of thousands of voices, all different pitches and tones echoed through my head. Each holding individual passion and excitement. It sounded like a large ocean wave of vocals and felt like a strong gust of wind filled with cheer. As I stood there alone, I tried my best to sink deeply into that very moment. I know I am not alone when I say that this feeling reminded me of being in another dimension. Many others who have traveled the world or lived abroad can attest to this feeling. Hearing the different languages and the various unique accents made me feel like I was an alien. In logical terms I was an alien residing in a country that was not my own. As I attempted to soak up that moment at Minibar, I was removed from those thoughts with a gentle nudge by my friend Veronica. As I slowly turn my head toward her, I could see both Patricia and her friend laughing. I redirected my attention toward Veronica who sweetly grabbed my hand and led me back to the group. As I walk toward them, I realized that Patricia, her friend and Veronica were all laughing at me! Veronica and Patricia's friend explained something in Spanish through the laughter, but I did not understand them.

Patricia then stepped in front of me slowly and said in English, "You were off in your own world. You are *morada* like your sister!" she stated with laughter still in her voice.

I chuckled in agreement because I was surely in a new world. Although I enjoyed basking in that moment while standing alone, I was equally embarrassed that I was caught by my friends. There were countless funny moments and silly situations this particular night.

For instance, when Conso A. approached the group to socialize with us I noticed something strange happening. We each recommenced to converse with Conso A. when all of a sudden, a nicely manicured hand quietly reached around Conso A's open purse and slowly removed her wallet. Seeing that Conso A. did not notice this action, I became a little confused and concerned. However, I soon realized that it was Patricia's hand. Catching on to Patricia's motive for this prank, I chuckled to myself and kept talking. A few moments later I approached Patricia with my translator in hand. I told her via translator that I found it funny how she sits and observes people. She then laughed and responded with the same translator,

"This is why I do not drink so I have a better time seeing people wrong. You have noticed I have stolen the wallet of Conso A. and she has not yet noticed," Patricia said with authority as she secretly pointed toward the wallet tucked in her hand. After I read this I burst into laughter as she joined me. We both stood watching in laughter together as Conso A. had yet to notice her missing wallet. We then spoke a little about my past in the military and her police duties. As I talked with friends, I noticed from a distance that Zipporah and Chelle were tipsy as they kept using phrases to randomly burst into song. Everyone around was entertained by their silliness, clapping and laughing along. After a few more drinks at Minibar, we decided to walk to a club. Entering the club, we instantly became aware that it was packed from wall to wall. The band was live, and it seemed to be a popular club for the younger crowd yet there were all ages this night. We found a vacant spot on the side next to the stage and danced until our feet hurt. Zipporah and Chelle left a little early because they had to catch the last train to Seville. I, Amos and the others stayed a little longer. After leaving the first club, everyone decided to move to the next club. Meanwhile, Amos, Patricia, her friend and I ended up getting separated from the original group. We all walked to the hotdog shop to order a midnight snack. Amos called and checked on the children as I sipped a cold bottle of water. Subsequently, we finished our snacks and walked toward the plaza in attempt to find the group. What we found instead was so much better! A full moon and the streets filled with beautiful Christmas lights. Patricia began to snap photos of Amos and me in front of an oversized, lit Christmas ornament. Immediately after the photos were taken, I could feel my phone vibrate as Isabel began to message me asking our whereabouts. I gave my phone to Patricia to translate for me. Patiently waiting for the next move, Patri's friend and I were comfortably resting our feet on a cozy bench in the plaza. Patri let Isabel know who she was and explained to young Isabel that we were all tired with aching feet and ready to go home. I explained to Patricia in English that before Amos and I were to go home, I needed to know that Isabel was safe and with her friends. With an exhausted demeanor I looked into Patricia's eyes and knew she completely understood what I was asking. She nodded her head in compliance and began to message Isabel. It was not until later that night at home that I interpreted the messages between Patricia and Isabel and realize an absolutely graceful term within the

Spanish culture: Patri told Isabel that I wanted to "descansa bien." Which translates as: "rest good" knowing that Isabel was ok. I smiled at the adorable photo Isabel sent of her and her friends to ensure she was content. This made me more comfortable and less anxious for I desired to leave for home knowing that (my little Spanish sister) Isabel was secure. Amos and I walked Patricia to her car and said our "good nights." I kissed Patricia on both cheeks as she offered us a ride. We politely declined but she persisted. We reassured her that our house was very close. As Amos and I walked home in good spirits, we both discussed the caps of the night and how we had a great time. It was a little past midnight by the time we arrived home and all I could think of was how I would feel tomorrow for Zipporah's housewarming party. "Round two, I guess," I whispered to myself.

Zipporah found a house not too far from where we lived and that made me grateful. I knew that eventually Zipporah would find her own place, but I didn't know how far that would place her from the family. Nevertheless, God saw a way to keep us all close, yet honoring our need to have space and time apart. I lived about a three- to five-minute walk away from a grocery store called Mercadona. This was the store we all depended on because it was very close, and they provided fresh and healthy options. Zipporah's house was also close to this Mercadona. It was a cute little quaint three-bedroom, two-bath home. A perfect size for her and perfect location for us all. This night was Zipporah's housewarming party with many of her new friends and family. When Amos and I arrived around eight thirty, we had time to help Zipporah finish with last-minute preparations.

As the guests began to arrive, I noticed that this was a very mixed crowd. Zipporah was a very social person as I mentioned before, and this was proof of that. She had friends from the airbase, Utrera and Seville all in one place. The ages ranged from eighteen to fifty-one, causing me to be amazed at the diversity of this group. I can remember listening and watching everyone as they laughed, danced and conversed in this small Spanish home. The atmosphere was filled with love, joy and happiness. I took this time to practice my Spanish when I overheard two friends from the younger crowd talking to one another. Most of the crowd that was here were those of Tina's closest friends that became close to Zipporah. They all spoke Spanish and only two of them spoke English well enough to hold a conversation with us. Listening closely, I could easily understand.

"Zipporah's sister speaks better Spanish than she does, don't you agree?" Rocio asked Antonio in Spanish as they both laughed to themselves.

"More or less," Antonio answered with doubt. This short conversation between them made me laugh and realize that my Spanish needed more work. This was my first time meeting the friends of Tina and now close friends of my sister. I would always hear great things about them from either Zipporah or Tina, which piqued my interest of them all.

Rocío is an absolute delight. She is young, intelligent, beautiful and kind. She is a college student and currently learning English. She has a calm, mature and timid spirit yet she was not afraid to communicate with my family and me in spite of the language barrier. Rocio is also a great flamenco dancer! Amos and myself spoke a little with her privately and we all had an instant connection. I was happy to meet Rocio and looked forward to getting to know her better in the future. A few friends from the base attended the party as well. There was Jessica, Toni and Terrance. Jessica is a mutual friend of our entire family and she is a very fun friend. She loved adventure and dancing, and was looking forward to the second half of the night where we would hit the clubs to groove. Toni and Terrance were a couple of two fresh years. Terrance is a Black American middle-aged man with great enthusiasm, humor, wisdom and pride. We met him through his wife, Toni, whom Zipporah and I also met at Gym Coliseum 94. Toni was quiet yet sassy and funny as well. She was a smaller figured woman yet fit, Filipino, with long dark hair. We enjoyed Toni a lot because she displayed loyalty and a desire to learn from us as we hoped to learn from her. We all continued to drink and laugh as Terrance made jokes about Zipporah's dancing. Nonetheless, the party turned out spectacular and everyone had a blast. Looking around I could perceive that every person in that room was a reflection of our growth and purpose here in Spain. Whether my past, present, or future I knew that every event I take part in will always be documented and embedded in my head and heart. Jessica was a reflection of both my past and my present. Jessica is a US military spouse. She's a Puerto Rican American with four beautiful children. Her husband, Karlos, is Puerto Rican as well. They are both from Virginia Beach and their marriage was that of a "best friend" type of partnership. Jessica constantly mentioned how impressed she was at how rapidly we became integrated with the locals. Talking throughout the night with Jessica assured me that she was definitely a future lifelong friend.

I laughed so hard that night that my abs ached. Our Afro-Dominican friend was there, and she played a prominent role in my amusement. Her name is Maria and she too was a mother. Maria was strong, stunning and brave. She spoke her mind and her sense of humor was outrageous. She displayed an aggressive personality yet a sweet attitude. When she and Zipporah got together it was like a live comedy show without props. They both screamed, giggled and danced the entire time. Our bonds as three strong international black women were unbreakable, and everyone could see that. As we prepared to leave the house and step into the streets, we all took shots of whiskey, saluting to our new life in Spain and our new friendships.

We all finally went out and danced. Toni and Terrance left early because Terrance had to work the next morning. We ended up at a lively club with a younger crowd that we nicknamed "The Dungeon." This club was large, dim and it possessed an antique design. The music was on point and we all danced all night. Isabel left first. Then the others slowly began to depart. Dominican Maria and Jessica left together because their homes were closer to one another. Amos and I were not far behind as we left shortly after Maria and Jessica. However, before I left, I pulled Antonio to the side.

"I'm going to my house, but please look after my sister," I asked him privately in Spanish.

Even though Antonio was the youngest of the group, he seemed to be one of the more mature ones. I could see in his eyes that he would honor my request and make sure Zipporah would be fine. Not to mention the fact that he adored Zipporah. So, I kissed all of our friends good night and Amos and I walked home. The night was yet another to add to my journal. Walking home with Amos, I expressed how proud I was of my sister for taking this life leap with us and flourishing so fast. She made friends, got her own place and already began to travel around Spain. Amos and I were happy to have our sister with us and I looked forward to the growth in our sisterhood and the future of our tribe.

Chapter 2:

Spain Through the Eyes of My Black American Children

I made it my top priority for the first few weeks that I arrived in Utrera, Spain, to get my children into a school. Amos and I wanted to ensure that they receive the full experience of Spain. My husband and I agreed that it was time for Amari to be admitted into the school system, yet as stated before I was not ready for Aaron to do so; therefore, my decision was not quite 100 percent until I first heard from God. Amari was eight years of age when we arrived in Spain and since he was four years of age, I homeschooled him. Amari was always mentally and spiritually ahead of his time and I believed the school system would not sculpt and mold him the way I, his mother, could and would.

However, I soon realized that my lack of faith in the school system was not that of all school systems but that of America's. I was raised by a college graduate and an educator, my mother, and by a man who lacked education yet thrived in society by owning his own business for over ten years, my father. My parents did not believe in the school system causing my mother to homeschool my siblings and me for about five years. This act of courage from my mother taught us all not just faith in God yet knowledge of our beautiful brown selves and many of our brown influencers who came before us. However, this soon changed due to financial reasons and my siblings and I were placed into public school. I remember the good times and the bad, but most importantly I remember the many lessons I learned that I could not have received from being homeschooled. For this very reason I chose to put Amari and my other two youngest in a charter school here in town. Nevertheless, this school had to be up to my motherly standards, and Salesianos was up to those standards and more. After deciding to allow Aaron to attend school as well, I made a conscious commitment to become greatly involved in my children's school lives. This was not hard seeing that Salesianos was a school that greatly encouraged parent involvement. I can recall the many projects, plays, meetings and activities that I participated in. Nevertheless, I enjoyed that change in my life and I was sure my children did as well. I knew in my mind and heart that my children would endure obstacles being not only new, American, and English speakers, but also black. From their skin color to their non-Catholic Christian beliefs to their hair texture and style. I knew that many parents and children would want to touch them. It sounds strange to a reader who has not lived abroad as a black family but through my past experiences of living in another country, I was aware of that future and I was ready to respond.

It was sometime after the Thanksgiving holiday when I first experienced Aaron being touched and admired for his different look. I had just picked Aaron up from his class and we headed to Amari's classroom for his pick-up, which was always about fifteen minutes after the younger children's. As we walked toward Amari's classroom, I noticed a group of mothers all huddled together. They were all respectfully and intensely listening to Stella, the mother of Amari's new friend Pelayo talking. As she continued her conversation with the ladies, her attention broke and Stella then slowly turned toward Aaron and me. When she first saw Aaron, her eyes lit up and she suddenly dropped to her knees with her arms stretched wide, welcoming Aaron into her embrace with love and adulation. Aaron let my hand go and dashed into her arms. She gently squeezed him while slowly standing to her feet. As Stella stood, the other mothers began to marvel at this lovely exchange. This love exchange between Stella and Aaron seemed to be a nonverbal invitation for the rest of the mothers to quench their curiosity. Consequently, all the mothers re-huddled around Stella and slowly began to touch and rub their fingers through Aaron's hair. Normally, I hate people touching my hair or my children's hair, but this moment felt a little different than other moments in the past. I realized that most of these mothers had never in their lives been close enough to a *"Negrito Americano"* to the point where they could feel the texture of our hair. So, there they were rubbing his hair with silent exclamations of acclaim.

This moment was both annoying yet beautiful at the same time. It reminded me of when we lived in Turkey. Many of the Turkish nationals would walk up to my son Amari who was only a baby at the time, and they would kiss his face. I always hated people doing that because I believed it to be slightly gross and rude. But in retrospect, I would rather a culture accept my family and me with love versus hate, and I felt love in that moment.

I was prouder and more impressed by Amari and Aaron every day as they flourished through their first year in school, learning, evolving, making new friends and throwing themselves into the change with gratitude. Thinking of Amari being my oldest child and a boy, I was expectant of his physical and mental changes. He had never attended school before, and I could tell it was becoming one of his favorite places to be. Amari blew our minds away as he learned the language so quickly and was picking up French as well. He made friends and companions very rapidly and that made me and Amos happy. For we worried about his maturity level and his will to remain strong and calm in pressing situations. Nonetheless, Amari consistently and confidently showed us differently. Many of the children Amari's age spoke to their parents as if they were their equal and Amari was taught against that. They also seemed to encounter more freedom, roaming the streets and bars in town as if they were adults. But this was the culture here and I respected it but I respected my beliefs as well and maintained my life teachings with my children.

An interesting observation about children in Spain is that in some ways they are very mature, especially the girls of course. Amari was only eight years old and I thought perhaps I had a little more time to prepare before he would come home talking about girls. Yet to my surprise I was incorrect. After about four months of living in Spain and attending school, I realized that Amari became comfortable enough with the language and culture to change his focus to something that I was not ready for: girls! One day, Amari came home and began to speak about how he really liked a girl named Greta in his class. I was a little startled to be honest. I can recall feeling a sense of fear yet interest as Amari talked about how nice Greta was. He claimed that she was not only smart but she was always willing to help him in school. As Amari's feelings continued to develop so did the friendship and bond between him and Greta. This resulted in our families becoming close as we all spent more time together. I remember a time that Greta and her parents came to our house to get Greta's hair braided. Greta saw that another girl in school had her hair braided by Zipporah, so she asked Amari if she could have hers braided. Amari was excited and did not hesitate to ensure this happened for his new crush. Being aware of the date, Amari generated an entire plan with D'iona's assistance, to ask little Greta to be his girlfriend. Zipporah and I tried to explain how he is young and should focus on friendship versus romance. His mind was not willing to comprehend or heed our advice; therefore, I did not pursue to continue. Because I understood the feeling, as I was once a little girl with a crush, I let him experience this moment and gave him advice when he needed it.

The school year continued and so did the parent involvement. Christmas was rapidly approaching as the school prepared for the big carol singing event and much more. My children all adored school and the many activities they were involved in. Their happiness was my joy, which gave me reliance and encouragement each day. December 17, 2018 was the date of the school's carol singing and all the children were full of eagerness. It was an annual event for the children in the elementary level to sing Christmas carols for the school staff and the parents. The younger children wore costumes of many kinds, created and designed by the parents. Aaron's class was dressed up as Christmas trees. They were all so cute! Cristina was kind enough to have Aaron's costume made by her mother-in-law and we were so grateful. Even though Aaron was not feeling well, I tried my hardest to doctor on him the night before because I knew how badly he wanted to participate. That morning I got him into his cute little Christmas tree costume instead of his regular school uniform and he looked extremely happy and cute. He had brown leggings, a green turtleneck, his beautiful Christmas tree costume, adorned with ornaments and glitter. Lastly, his hat was a gold star to top everything off. As I walked Aaron to his classroom, everyone stared at him in astonishment. I dropped him at his class, and I headed to the school's church where the children would be performing. As the staff and children all scurried around to complete last preparations, the door remained closed as all the parents waited in anticipation.

Waiting at the door with the rest of the parents of the church, I could hear the many accents of the parents speaking to one another with excitement. Instantaneously, my local Spanish friends began to point out an American family in front of us. I quickly turned in the direction of their fingers and proceeded to introduce myself to the husband. This American family was Karlos and Jessica. I remember feeling relief when I met them as we all spoke our language comfortably, laughing and making plans to get our children together. We exchanged contact information and gave traditional kisses. This meeting with Karlos and Jessica soon became a close family bond.

The doors finally opened and we all swiftly swarmed into the auditorium racing for the best front seats. The inside of the church was gorgeous! Lights, music, and decorations filled every space. When Aaron came out with his class I was a little nervous. But when they began to sing and dance, Aaron lit up as he knew every word of every song and he surprisingly perfected every dance move. He was enjoying himself so much despite his small cold. At that moment, I became slightly emotional because I saw how Aaron was changing, improving, progressing, and socializing! This was simply amazing to me and I wanted Amos to see; therefore, like most of the other parents I pulled out my phone and began to record every moment of my son's performance.

Like Charles Dickens once wrote, "It was the best of times, it was the worst of times." The best of my children's times here in Spain definitely outweighed the worst of times. But when those worst of times appeared it made me upset, yet each time taught me many lessons. I knew that Amari would have children who loved him and children who would hate him. Not only because of his personality flaws, or his willpower to be the best, but simply because he was different. Amari's first conflict was with a small, troubled boy named Paco. Amari encountered many difficult situations with this boy and many times I wanted to intervene. However, I knew it was important for him to learn lessons through these experiences with Paco so I and Amos would give him advice on how to handle bullies.

The first time that I heard about Paco Gomez was on a particular day at school when I went to retrieve Amari. He came down his classroom stairs crying and I instantly wanted to know what was wrong. As we slowly walked out toward home, Amari explained how a boy from his class hit him for no reason. Amari continued to expound on the situation as he stated that Paco meant to hit another boy but the boy dodged and Paco Gomez's punch landed on my son's face. I told him to suck it up and to use his God-given strength to defend himself next time. As we walked down the alley I could hear someone approaching. A little sweet voice began to scream in our direction.

"Amari! ¡Que te pasa! ¿Estas bien?" It was Natalia and her daughter Greta walking toward us. Greta had told her mother what happened and they wanted to check on Amari. We slowly walked down the alley toward home as Greta had her arm around Amari. Then Natalia turned to me and attempted to explain the situation. She slowly expounded in Spanish how the boy was troubled and had behavioral issues. As I attentively listened I could discern that Natalia recognized the "heartwarmth" in my eyes. She then began to explain how sympathetic Greta is and how concerned she was when she saw what had occurred between her new best friend and this troubled boy. I was appreciative of both Natalia and her daughter Greta for their love and concern. Consequently, Amari claimed that this was the moment when he fell in love with Greta. Hearing these words coming out of the mouth of my firstborn gave me goosebumps, but I was also proud that he valued women at such a young age. Amari is respectful, loving, gentle and sweet. These characteristics of Amari make other boys jealous and he had to learn how to defend himself mentally, physically and verbally. Amos saw fit to teach Amari a few defensive moves to help him become more confident when conflict arises.

Amari has made many friends and we allow him to be free to spend time with them. Whether he is at the park, pool, or in the center, I noticed that Amari was having a little trouble with bullies. Some were older, some younger and others his age. Meanwhile, Paco Gomez was becoming a thorn in Amari's side. His behavioral or mental disability seemed to excuse him from certain disciplinary actions that other children received. When Amari first started school his father had a heart-to-heart conversation with him. One of the main facts that Amos wanted Amari to understand was that many people will like him, but others will not. Over the course of stories that Amari shared with me about Paco Gomez, it seemed apparent that Paco Gomez was envious of my son, or perhaps he wanted to be friends with Amari but because of his behavioral issues, he did not know how to express that desire to Amari. It is difficult to know with children. After the first time Paco hit Amari, Amos warned him to always be on guard with this particular child. Amari complied because weeks later he shared with me how Paco walked up to Amari in the middle of class. All of the other children quietly watched as they knew and anticipated what was coming. Paco Gomez stretched his neck, arms and knuckles as if he were about to enter a fight. He then wound his arm back in preparation to punch Amari as hard as he could. However, as Paco's fist came close, Amari firmly caught his swing. For a few seconds

Amari squeezed Paco's fist as he contemplated the idea of hitting Paco in the face. Instead, Amari forcefully threw his fist down as to nonverbally say, "Don't mess with me." After this exchange Paco Gomez slowly walked back to his seat. Iván Luis, one of Amari's closest classmates watched with his mouth wide open, along with many of the other students in the class. Then Greta abruptly started to chant Amari's name. "Amari! Amari!" Greta chanted with pride as other children joined her. The entire class was now chanting Amari's name in reverence to him standing up against Paco Gomez. Amari exclaimed to me that this moment was when he realized Greta had a crush on him as well. When Amari made that statement it took me by surprise because he did not sound like an eight-year-old boy to me. He sounded like a young man who was in love; still it was a little scary. I had bittersweet feelings toward hearing about Amari's struggles with bullies; nevertheless, I was optimistic about my son and his willpower to remain persistent in his need to fight back with words and only with fists if it was necessary. Amos and I have always informed Amari that fighting should be a last resort when confronted with issues with another child or young adult.

Amari also told me of a time when Paco Gomez taunted all of the boys from the class. He was calling out the names but changing the words from masculine to feminine so as to insult their pride.

"Eduarda, Pelaya, Ivána Luisa," Paco Gómez began to tease. One of the boys, Eduardo, attempted to fight back and responded with a name of his own.

"Paca," Eduardo stated with force and pride.

He knew he had won this battle, but Paco was quick with his brain and replied with

"Eduardita."

With embarrassment in his eyes, Eduardo gave up as he shrugged in aggravation. Meanwhile, Paco Gomez saved Amari for last.

"Amara," Paco taunted.

"Pacía," Amari responded.

"Amarita," Paco hastily replied.

"Pacita," Amari calmly responded.

Thinking hard at this point Paco boastfully stated, "Amaritita."

Amari, still confident knowing that he had a few more in his pocket replied, "Pacitilita."

The room grew silent as all the boys watched with expectancy. Paco acknowledged with nothing and walked away in defeat. My spirit jumped up and down inside as if I was watching a basketball game and my team was winning. I was so proud of my son for not giving into the ignorance of this boy, yet he defended not only himself but his friends and the other boys in the class. His win was all of their wins.

Although Amari came across some immature bullies, he also acquired many friends. The friends that Amari chose were good children and they all possessed loyalty. Amari's closest classmate and friend was Iván Luis, and he was a good boy. He was sweet and stylish yet timid. However, Iván Luis was also strong and sure of himself and I believe that is what attracted them to one another. I was happy to know that Amari spent most of his time at school with well-behaved children. I was equally ecstatic about the loyalty of his friends even when an issue was presented before them. For example, one afternoon Amari came to me angry, with a tremble in his voice.

"Paco Gomez is trying to turn my best friend Iván Luis against me," Amari announced to both D'iona and me.

Surprised yet confused at the words that he chose, I preceded him with a question: "Why do you say that Amari?"

"Because yesterday at school I heard him whispering to Iván Luis, 'You do not need to play with Amari because he is very bad.'"

"Lie! He is very good," Iván Luis responded with frustration yet passion in his voice.

I adored little gentle Iván Luis even more than I had before after Amari shared this story with me. I explained to Amari that he should not allow the lies of a troubled child to worry his mind. I elaborated on the fact that he had good friends and situations will arise to show Amari who is loyal and true to him and who is not. Amari understood and became relieved to know that he had a good friend. This same incident occurred with Amari's other two friends Pelayo and Greta. Nevertheless, Paco Gomez was once again shot down with rejection as Pelayo and Greta denied his lie with loyalty and love for their friend Amari. As Amari persisted to tell me stories of Paco, I knew that he would continue to have problems with this child; therefore, I made a conscious decision to talk to the mother of Paco Gomez. I was getting tired of hearing about this boy harassing my child. For he was tireless with these harassments but he did know the anger and rage of a hurt black boy. I believe that Paco Gomez learned that words are Amari's weakness. You see, Amari has always had issues with controlling his anger in the past, even as a toddler. He has always possessed a short fuse and this ran through my mind consistently as I would hear about Paco's taunts. However, Amari is like a "gentle giant." He is a little sensitive and does not like to fight. He was physically built like his father, which is extremely thick and strong. One aspect about Amari is that he knows the strength that he possesses and tries his hardest not to use it. Instead, he displays his anger through tears, his artwork or acting out. Sometimes in the past he would even growl to release his anger. This was an unhealthy display of anger in my opinion and I wanted Amari to learn to control that energy. We taught our children that emotions are genetically designed into our being purely for survival, that we must use those emotions and respond in the right way. On the other hand, as I view this situation with positivity, I am extremely grateful for the role that Paco Gomez played in Amari's life. Because I believe that Paco's behavior was teaching Amari how to stay cool and control his anger. What angered Amari the most were the jokes Paco Gomez would make about his mother. I'm assuming it is a universal unwritten rule that mother jokes are no jokes at all. Paco Gomez said something to Amari about being the "son of a bitch." Amari felt an immediate flash of anger overcome him.

In response, Amari took one big step into Paco Gomez's face and loudly growled: "STOP!" As Amari stood in front of Paco, he began to tighten his fist in rage.

Suddenly, Iván Luis steps in between them and proceeded to warn Amari. "No, no, no! He is crazy," Iván Luis proclaimed in dismay. For he could see that his best friend was becoming irate with Paco Gomez. Both Pelayo and Eduardo repeated the same thing. They warned Amari not to hit him back because he was crazy. Understanding what his friends were trying to portray, Amari calmed himself down and angrily walked away instead of punching Paco Gomez for insulting me, his mother.

Each incident between Amari and Paco made Amari suppress his anger and walk away. Thus, making Amari an overall better version of himself. One day I even voiced to Amari that I met Paco's mother and wanted to inform her of this harassment from her son. Amari replied with disagreement. He convinced me that he can fight his own battles and handling Paco Gomez had become easier now that he has learned of his condition.

For months now I have been concerned about Amari and his relationship with Paco Gomez. Today Amari came home and told me what happened between them. Amari explained how Paco Gomez "came for Greta." In other words, Paco Gomez tried to hurt Greta. Amari and Greta were sitting together in class and working. Out of nowhere, Paco Gomez slowly walked up to Greta while cracking his knuckles in preparation to hit her. He lifted his tightly clenched fist and took a hard swing at Greta. Greta quickly hunched over her desk and covered her head in a fetal position to protect herself from the impact of Paco's fist. Before his punch landed on Greta, Amari quickly grabbed and blocked his arm. Without thinking Amari quickly punched Paco Gomez in the face! Shocked and angry Paco Gomez walked away holding his face in pain.

"Oh, thank you, Amari!" Greta expressed with a blush. While my family and I do not condone violence, except in self-defense, I must admit that I was secretly proud of Amari for standing up for his friend. I could feel that Amari had enough of Paco's ways no matter if he was mentally sick or not. His attempt to hurt his friend would not pass in his history. From that day forward I heard less about Paco Gomez. I felt relief from this manner knowing that my son was learning and growing. I did not want to worry about Amari so much and needed to focus on getting D'iona into school.

It was New Year 2019 and six months since we arrived in Spain. Abi's Spanish lessons with Tina were going very well, Aaron was embedded into his school routine better than we expected and Amari was learning extremely rapidly. My children were becoming more mature each day and they were adapting well to the culture and change of Spain. This made me nostalgic; however, I was concerned about my little princess D'iona. Now, playing the role of her mother and Amos the role of her father, brought up many obstacles. Not only was D'iona not in school, but she was also displaying overly sensitive behavior. Before I agreed to take D'iona for a year to help my older sister, Keturah, I prayed about it. Not only did God answer my prayer but he also gave me the strength to endure this challenge. D'iona was at a crossroads in Spain. She was three years older than Amari, placing her as the oldest child in the home; this was a major change for D'iona seeing as though she was the only child my eldest sister, Keturah, bore. In reality this change and the various others were complicated and frustrating at times for her. She hated sitting at home all day with Abi, she missed her mother dearly and she was not adapting well to Spain. Discerning D'iona's spirit I came to the conclusion that she was not truly happy and would never be without her mother. I understood this greatly and worked diligently with my husband and Zipporah to ensure D'iona was loved and accepted here. D'iona expressed that she enjoyed her time with her cousins, and she liked living in Spain, but she wanted to attend school. D'iona was raised going to public school; therefore, this was her longest time other than summer breaks, that she was out of school. D'iona is a wise, intelligent and funny little queen and I relished having her here with us in Spain. Due to the circumstances with my sister, the paperwork needed to register D'iona for school was wildly delayed. Nonetheless, I was determined to execute my plan to get my princess in school, so I decided to find another route. With the help from my local friends here in town I was able to achieve that goal. D'iona started school about a week after I submitted the paperwork requested and she was cheerful. Not only did Salesianos find a slot for DD, we also received uniforms from another parent that fit DD perfectly and were all like new. D'iona was scheduled to be in the fifth grade but the school informed me that her birthdate legally placed her in the 6th grade. This made me and DD nervous, nevertheless it had to be achieved and that it was.

After a few weeks of DD attending school, I can recall that my meeting with her teacher was approaching. I was very proud of myself for taking the initiative to make this happen, and for that reason and others I was excited to meet the person who would be teaching D'iona. After D'iona's first day of school her teacher, Celeste Martinez, made sure to set up a teacher-parent conference with me. I marked the date on my calendar and prepared myself. The day of the conference I got dressed, ensured the children were all bathed, and prepared their uniforms for the next day. I headed to the school a little early since I knew I was not aware of how to get to DD's class. I then was forced to video chat with D'iona in order for her to guide me to the classroom; it was sort of comical. Finally arriving with DD's help, I greeted Celeste with the traditional kisses. To my observation she was a very pleasant woman. I was actually a bit surprised at how well she spoke English, while at the same time relieved. One of the first aspects of her life of which she shared with me was that in her past she lived in America for four years. Wondering what state, I asked her politely and she replied with Fort Worth, Texas. I thought to myself, Wow, out of all places, Fort Worth, Texas, a place where both DD and her mother lived for years. She started our meeting by asking me to share a little bit of D'iona's situation and background. Celeste wanted a better understanding of D'iona for this would better assist her in teaching this young American girl who only speaks English. Ms. Martinez reassured me that she was not prying yet asking genuinely to help. I proceeded to explain the circumstance of D'iona. We then spoke about DD's status as together we brainstormed solutions. She was a little concerned about D'iona's shyness, but I assured her that DD would become a completely different child when she became more comfortable in her environment. As I mentioned previously, D'iona is very intelligent and wise, and I was very confident in her progression living here in Spain. Finally, our conversation slowly shifted to our life stories as we both became more content with one another. I also found it angelic, coincidental and slightly comical that Celeste was chosen to be the teacher for D'iona. Curious to know more about Celeste Martinez's life in America, I began to question her. She gladly shared her experiences with me, and I mine. She explained her toughest moments and how it was difficult for her to connect with the Americans. This was a common statement I heard from many other Spanish people. The majority of Spaniards with whom I conversed about their experience living or visiting the United States have expressed negatively about the people. They believed many Americans are closed and hard to connect with. This I agreed with to a certain extent. I would always say, "You cannot judge many by a few." It was then that I realized how important it was for me to connect with this particular teacher. We continued to enjoy our conversation, but the meeting was ending. We exchanged numbers and made plans to convene again. I was happy to know that D'iona's teacher was an intelligent, open-minded, kind, understanding, and experienced person. She was what D'iona needed.

It was D'iona's second week of school and she was absolutely loving it! She was making so many friends and they were happy to assist her. She was specifically ecstatic about Valentine's Day and the many activities planned for the school. This particular day was Valentine's and Amari came to me in maturity to inform me that he desired to buy roses for his crush. So I asked him how many roses he desired to purchase. He said three. Before purchasing the roses for Amari I challenged him to solve an equation, a thing I always did with Amari when I was homeschooling him. He needed to solve the equation before I would give him the euros. I wanted my children to become independent and knowledgeable of everyday routines. I began with the question as Amari and I stood on the sidewalk across from the rose stand.

"If the seller were selling each rose for two euros a piece and you want three, how many euros do you need?"

He applied thought to the equation then began to solve it.

"Three roses times two euros each"—Amari began to ponder more—"equals six euros, I need six euros!" he proclaimed with excitement.

I smiled at him with pride and rewarded his correct answer with the six euros. Amari approached an older gypsy man selling roses at a corner and purchased his three roses. Later on that day, I asked Amari how things went with the roses and Greta. He told me that Greta was both surprised and appreciative. I asked D'iona how was her day with the school activities and she replied by showing me a bag full of Valentine's treats while Aaron watched eating the candy he received. Abi reached for some of D'iona's candy and D'iona politely allowed her to proceed. The children all experienced a beautiful and exciting day and that made me content.

My husband and I did not celebrate holidays much, but we allowed our children to enjoy their youth by participating in the various festivities of each holiday. Utrera is a lively town with many celebrations; one of it's most treasured qualities. I appreciated the family ethics here and the mandatory need to place the children first. The children of Utrera displayed signs of cheerfulness whenever I would observe them at the park, restaurants, or simply outdoors playing and socializing with each other. My two youngest were like glue sticks to me our first year here, but Amari became deeply embedded into the routine and ways of Utrera. Most days he was allowed to hang with friends as long as his homework was completed and on most weekends. Not only did he develop friendships at school, but he also made them outside school. In the winter season Amari's favorite place to go was the park. On most weekends he would stay out all evening. D'iona was more of a homebody; therefore, most days she would be in the house with me. After many evenings and nights of Amari venturing to the park, I began to hear stories about another bully. I became outraged hearing of his encounters with this particular boy. Yet I remained faithful and calm as Amari would share with me his endeavors. This boy apparently lived in our local neighborhood. The first time Amari saw him he was headed home. He was walking home alone from the local park and he saw a family passing him. He noticed a boy around his age glaring at him. Amari simply stared back at him.

Suddenly the little boy raised both arms and says, "What's up, dickhead?" in his Andalusian accent.

I loved that my son was becoming more independent and fluent in the language; however, I never wanted him to learn bad words or experience this type of behavior from another child. But I knew that it was his journey and would only toughen him up. Furthermore, hearing Amari imitate this boy as he dramatized each scene, honestly gave me an urge to burst into laughter. Thinking upon my past with humor I can recall hearing this disrespectful greeting in my own old neighborhood growing up and that tickled me. Amari responded by simply rolling his eyes and kept walking.

Amari's second encounter with this boy caused Amari to come home holding his ear in pain. I asked him what happened and he reluctantly told me the story. Amari was playing soccer with his friends at the park and the same boy approached Amari while he was alone on the field. They stared each other down. The boy inched closer. Suddenly Amari felt a sharp pain in his right ear! The boy executed some sort of "high-kick karate move" on Amari. Amari grabbed his left ear in pain and the boy saw the opportunity to pursue his physical abuse toward my son. He firmly punched Amari in the stomach with force in his fist and hatred in his eyes. Amari hunched over, holding his stomach in pain as he slowly arose. Within half of a second, Amari felt a surge of anger volt through his entire body. He paused his attempt to rise, turned to this pale boy, lifted his right arm high, and punched the boy in his stomach as hard as his anger would allow. Caught off guard by the impact of Amari's punch, the boy doubled over in pain. He seemed as though he wanted to cry from the pain, but his pride would not allow him to do so in front of Amari. The boy swiftly shifted his head the other way and quickly walked away while still hunched over, holding his stomach in pain.

    By this time, I became nervous about Amari going to the park alone. I told D'iona that she is Amari's older cousin and I wanted her to make an effort to accompany him to the park more often. The third time Amari encountered the boy was when he went to the park with D'iona. They ran into a group of older teenage girls who were all intrigued by Amari and D'iona. This group wanted to feed their curiosity; therefore, they became friendly with Amari and D'iona, asking many questions. Meanwhile, the boy noticed the attention that Amari was receiving. Instead of staying to himself, the boy used this attention as an opportunity to embarrass Amari. He slowly inched his way toward Amari as he watched on edge. Not knowing what to expect Amari shifted his position in a defensive stance. Finally, the boy drew close enough to seemingly walk past Amari. But as the boy walked past Amari he purposely brushed his shoulders against Amari's with aggression. Amari stood his ground and attempted to ignore the boy once again. Creeping slowly behind my son, the boy then reached quietly to push Amari. However, Amari caught his arm in anticipation and angrily threw it down. The teenage girls did not notice the boy and asked Amari why he was so upset. To them, his anger seemed misplaced or unwarranted. He quickly calmed down and explained what happened. The girls seemed to have known about the behavior of this particular child. They assured Amari that soon he would get bored. Amari was getting fed up with this boy for he was not a coward.

I was beginning to second-guess my decision to move to such a small town as I pondered nervously about Amari's bully experiences. I wanted to magically make those particular events disappear in my son's life's journey but it was not possible. I began to question if it was healthy for my son to be in a place that lacks diversity. Nevertheless, I thought of my goals for my children and reassured myself that this was not forever. I needed to be strong and brave for my family as obstacles arose and that I did. One day Amari was walking alone to the park when he ran into a large *pandilla* of ten to twelve teenagers.

"Look at this little *jit* (runt)!" Amari heard one of them express in their native slang. Amari knew that they were speaking about him.

Suddenly, they all began to chant loudly, *"Vete para África!* Go back to Africa!" This group of teenagers became more obnoxiously loud, eventually yelling.

Amari said he felt both angry and annoyed. "Because I didn't even do anything wrong, Mommy!" Amari professed in agitation.

My heart broke as Amari made this statement, but he ignored them and proceeded to the park and that was a sign of strength in my eyes. His father explained to him how Utrera is a small town and many of the teenagers are not used to seeing diversity. I realized that they were only teenagers, still children, as I visualized myself slapping them all. However, as a mother I would do anything to protect my children. When Amari told Amos and me about this particular incident, I had to hold back my anger and tears. These teenagers first acknowledged the fact that Amari is young. However, this did not stop them from verbally attacking him simply because of the color of his skin. I was disappointed that my son had to face the reality of racism and misjudgment. My personal opinion is that the teenagers were simply ignorant cowards. They are ignorant to assume that Amari is African just because he is brown. And they are cowards to verbally attack a young child. We made Amari understand that eventually people like those teenagers would face the consequences of their actions.

"The battle is not mine, it's the Lord's," Amari quoted with encouragement.

Later that night after tucking the children into bed, Amos and I conversed about this situation. We were both very relieved and grateful for Amari and how he handled the entire situation.

He was not traumatized by it nor did he lose his motivation to keep making new friends. In fact, when he first arrived home from the park that night, he did not even mention the incident. He was forced to elaborate on his thoughts when D'iona mentioned something that reminded him of the incident. I will admit that his story hurt my feelings as a young Black American mother much more than it hurt Amari as a young Black American boy. Amos made sure he reiterated to Amari that this was a prime example of how some people will like and accept us, while others may not. Amos encouraged Amari to never allow anything or anyone to stop him from shining or being a great person. Amari was learning so many valuable life lessons at such a young age. As their father spoke, all the children listened diligently and I believe they all learned a valuable lesson from Amari and his experience. Sometimes it's the things you don't do that outweigh the things you do. For example, Amari's neighborhood bully later became a friend of all three of our children.

As Amari's bully stories decreased, my children's school schedule increased. It was my pleasure to become an active mother in the school community, yet it was also hectic at times with three children attending. Walking to and from school five days a week, four times a day had its pros and cons. The cons are obvious, but the most valued pro is watching Aaron evolve. Over the course of time, I have literally watched the transformation of communication and comprehension between Aaron and his teacher. I have even seen how it has transpired into our home as his communication has improved tremendously. I believe that Celia is simply an amazing teacher. Her English is limited; thus, when Aaron first entered her classroom she used her body language, gestures and the little English that she knew to communicate. But she used less English and more Spanish over the course of time. The body language transformed into small Spanish phrases. Eventually, she spoke more and more Spanish to Aaron. His little mind quickly absorbed the language and eventually she spoke fluent Spanish to Aaron and he understood most if not all. To see Aaron and his teacher advance from limited communication to total communication was beautiful. Nonetheless, there were times when I was worried about Aaron's anxieties being displayed during school. I developed routine phases for Aaron whenever he would have an episode and I needed to inform Celia of this. However, I was not confident in my Spanish speaking abilities to be able to communicate these routines to her and help her understand why. Thus, I became perplexed and nervous as I pondered on how to tell Aaron's teacher. For weeks, I struggled with how to explain to her Aaron's quirks. I questioned myself if I should ask for a one-on-one meeting with Don Carlos to translate or ask a friend like Vanessa or Celeste to help me translate. I also thought to just speak to her myself with the little Spanish I possessed. After several weeks passed, I was able to gather the confidence to speak to Celia. One evening I approached her alone in the classroom while Aaron played with a friend. I slowly began to attempt to explain everything to her in Spanish, yet, it was not necessary. As I stuttered over words and translations I noticed that Celia was finishing my sentences for me. I was relieved, happy and surprised all at once. "Wow," I whispered to myself. This woman learned Aaron as well as a mother would know their own child. In that moment I felt that Celia was an angel sent to teach my child.

Later that evening, I explained my observation to my husband and his response was simple. "Salesianos is one of the best schools in this region. Of course they hire the best teachers. The cream of the crop," Amos responded with humor.

I laughed as I thought to myself, that my husband was 100 percent correct. All of my children's teachers were cream of the crop. While I completely agree with his response, I knew there was a little more to that observation. Aaron's teacher Celia was using her spiritual intuition to better understand the children and how to handle them all. I believe that she is a powerful woman and has the respect of her students and their parents. I witnessed, on the first day when Celia accepted the challenge to teach a boy from a different country, culture and mind. She did it with love and grace. She used every resource in her mind to make it work between Aaron and her although it may have been challenging. I then began to appreciate my time more retrieving Aaron from school as I watched him comply confidently with all instructions given to him in Spanish. Celia treated every one of her students as if they were her own child. But I always felt as though she had a special love for Aaron because of his need for more attention than the other children. This I believe helped Aaron develop a close and trusting bond with his teacher. I often wondered how Ms. Celia felt about having a child in her class on the autistic spectrum. I questioned this about her to myself ... Was she nervous, reluctant, excited or discouraged? Nonetheless, I loved this teacher for Aaron and would always include her, Amari's teacher, and D'iona's teachers in my prayers.

It was the beginning of March and time was moving fast. The children were all doing well in school, but today was the day I would find out how well academically they all were actually doing. I was vaguely concerned about Amari and Aaron's report and honestly terrified about D'iona's. I attended the progress meetings for Amari then Aaron as I nervously dreaded attending D'iona's. I did not know what to expect from D'iona academically, whereas her mother knew and exclaimed that she was very bright in school. Nevertheless, this was a Spanish-speaking charter school and D'iona started six months late in a grade above her level. I knew she was making friends and catching on fast to the routine of school. Nevertheless, I wanted to know more. As I quietly and anxiously sat on a beautifully designed bench in the courtyard of the school, I attempted my hardest to fight the nervousness and negative thoughts of D'iona's progress report. It was approximately six thirty and I hurried through the somewhat dark hallways of the school to meet her teacher. Suddenly I was stopped by Celeste, D'iona's teacher. She frantically asked me to come back downstairs and patiently wait on the bench as she went to get the results. After escorting me downstairs to wait, Celeste hurried back up the stairs to retrieve the test results and opinions of D'iona's other teachers. This news alone made me even more nervous than before. D'iona is an extremely mature and wise child on one hand. However, it was true that sometimes she lacked enthusiasm in academics. I tried to be more lenient with her because I knew that D'iona had many odds stacked against her. To give you an illustration, D'iona's separation from her mother, the struggle of learning a second language, skipping a grade as well as her phase of adolescents. The school informed me that due to D'iona's birthday, her age places her in the sixth grade. This posed a problem as D'iona would have been in the fifth grade in America. Consequently, D'iona had attended school for over a month in Spain. One month in my opinion could not fully assess a child's full potential, but simply their progress. During the assessment process, each teacher was mandated to test D'iona's comprehension level. I and Amos knew for a fact that D'iona was more than capable of not only succeeding but excelling in the sixth grade. However, she could only prosper if she applies herself. Amos and I had countless loving conversations with D'iona about this very aspect of herself and many others. I continued to wait for Ms. Celeste as I was writing down my thoughts and feelings in my journal.

My writing suddenly comes to an abrupt halt as I felt a slight nudge on my shoulder. It was Celeste. As my cloudy thoughts began to clear in my head, I began to clearly hear that she was ready. She was accompanied by another woman whom she introduced to me as the school counselor. The counselor greeted me with the traditional Spanish kiss and that put me at ease. I immediately noticed their energy of teamwork and determination. We went upstairs to the classroom and as we began the meeting I realized the counselor did not speak any English. Celeste patiently translated the entire meeting and I was impressed. The majority of D'iona's progress report was focused on her behavior, which lacked enthusiasm. Both Celeste and the counselor wanted to know more about D'iona and her background so that they could better assist her in her needs. I explained the dynamic of my role in D'iona's life and why. I elaborated on how D'iona really missed her mother and was having a difficult time adjusting. The following conversation that I had with these two women in my opinion was divine.

The teachers all agreed that D'iona lacked motivation and her depression of being separated from her mother was affecting her schooling. Their best solution was to allow D'iona to stay with her sixth-grade class. However, she would be receiving extra help and tutoring. The teachers also agreed that D'iona should focus solely on learning Spanish. They wanted her to heal from her past and deal with her emotions. They wanted her focus to be solely on learning the language as then she would be able to catch up academically.

I was a little frustrated because I felt as though they should have put my niece in the fifth grade to begin with. But I was grateful that the school was willing to accommodate and work with her. The counselor and Celeste then began giving me tips on how to help D'iona. In the end, the meeting left me feeling discouraged yet grateful. Discouraged because I felt as though I had failed as a guardian and aunt and grateful because Salesianos was so willing to help us as a family. They embraced my children and accepted the diversity as they learn from our culture and we theirs. Celeste, the sweet counselor and I came up with a plan to help D'iona. That night I spoke with her mother, my husband and Zipporah. I informed them of D'iona's progress and explained what was discussed in the meeting. I then had an additional conversation with D'iona. I reiterated what I mentioned to her before, that I wanted to see more initiative from her. I challenged D'iona and told her that I wanted her to dig deep and learn Spanish as if her life depended on it. She understood and promised me that she would do better and work harder. After this conversation, I noticed an improvement from D'iona. The sense of care and community that the school presented amazed me. They viewed each child as a jewel. They came up with a customized plan for not only D'iona, but for Aaron as well. They viewed the children as individuals instead of a number like many of the school systems in America do.

The end of this school year for the children was extremely busy but fun. Our family tribe was growing and everyone was in good spirits. D'iona, Amari and Aaron were all preparing for their end of school year dance as well as the school procession. Earlier in the school year Don Carlos approached me with Don Cristobal. They politely explained that they were aware and respected that our family are non-Catholic Christians. However, there was a very special and traditional dance coming up in which they wanted Amari to participate. Amari had a good reputation for his dancing and rhythm throughout the school, which I assumed could be vital to this dance. Don Carlos, the administrative leader asked if I was comfortable with Amari dancing for the school procession. This specific dance is called *Lo Seises* and it seemed special for the young boys who were selected to perform. To my understanding, Lo Seises is a traditional Catholic dance that dates as far back as the fourteenth century. It was originally just six cathedral boys who performed the dance but over the years changed to ten boys. They performed their dance at the cathedral in front of the high altar to honor God. This custom is known throughout Spain but is focalized in Seville.

I asked Amari if he wanted to participate.

"Of course," Amari responded in his Andalusian accent.

He intelligently explained to me that he felt honored and privileged to be asked to dance in this traditional event. He also mentioned that it would be an awesome cultural learning experience for him. I was very proud of Amari for having such a mature outlook on our experiences here in Spain. He was embracing the culture and pressing through the challenges as well.

Amari and the other nine boys practiced twice a week for four months in preparation. Four of them were Amari's closest classmates and friends. They all did a great job working together to keep a steady rhythm. The dance was very strange as well as difficult. It appeared to be based mainly on rhythm and unison. The dance consisted of the boys forming two parallel lines of five boys. They slowly begin the dance by taking steady yet rhythmic steps. Each step is followed by a lift with their toes. Their hands were neatly folded behind their backs. They started down the center hall of the church and slowly made their way to the front center after church, ending in front of the school director. It was the center where they faced each other and begin to change their direction. This caused the boys to interlock and pass each other and switch sides. This was repeated numerous times while the children's choir music played.

The attire of the boys was spectacular! The design consisted of old fashion white mid-length britches, a large old-fashioned white shirt and a silk, sky-blue vest laced with gold. There was also a matching blue and gold trim belt with a white shawl to go over their shoulders. They all wore white stockings and white, flat yet fancy shoes. Their magnificent attire was finalized with a large fitting matching blue and white hat laced with gold with a beautiful large blue feather in the front. Our boys looked amazing! As the mother's watched, some became emotional.

The boys performed this dance three separate times during the designated week before the procession. The first performance was on Thursday and the second performance was Friday evening at the church of Salesianos. I stood silently observing the boys as I noticed the many people crowded in and around church just to see the same. Us parents of the boys were seated in the front, labeled reserved. As the boys began to dance I intensely watched their every move. My heart was filled with pride and joy as I focused most of my attention on Amari. Looking into the faces of the other parents, I could see the emotional overload. I then turned in the direction of the other mothers as I witnessed their red faces and wet eyes dripping. The other mothers Stella, Emilia and Isabel were all standing there gazing and overcome with sentiment. Tears were falling from their faces as they watched gripping their hands.

The boy's third and last performance was during the school procession. The procession began at the church and all of the small children were dressed up as angels, while the designated men carried the depiction of Jesus Christ on the cross. It seemed as though every person in Utrera was out that evening to view this procession. I accompanied Aaron along with the other parents accompanying their children, all dressed as beautiful blue and white angels. One of the mothers of Aaron's class, María José, was kind enough to let me borrow an angel costume as I didn't possess one or have the time or skill to prepare one. The costume was silk sky-blue trimmed with silver glitter fabric. His wings were made of cardboard covered with white feathers. I especially loved his halo, made of white fur sitting on top of his beautiful locs(hair). The parents and I accompanied our angels as we watched them walk and play with one another. I specifically remember walking past a very old couple and hearing the wife say to her husband,

"Look at the black angel."

I do not prefer for my children or myself to be described as "black" by others outside of our race. Nonetheless, I could discern that this woman was speaking with admiration and adornment, not hate or disrespect. She was simply observing the beauty and uniqueness of my little angel Aaron. Aaron really enjoyed himself at this occasion and it was nice watching him play with his little friends. Meanwhile, Amos stayed with Amari as Lo Seises boys walked the procession as well. Zipporah, Keturah, Meli, D'iona and Abi all watched from the side of the street with many other people of the town. Here, they were able to capture beautiful pictures and videos of the event.

It was as though my faith grew overnight as well as my ability to speak things as they are. I was missing my eldest sister, Keturah, and so was her daughter and Zipporah. When Keturah arrived with her new partner, Meli Rosa, I was a little apprehensive because I did not know this woman. However, I was also faithful and willing to make the acquaintance, in hopes it becomes a sisterhood. They came to stay, and I was happy that our tribe was growing and that D'iona was finally reunited with her mother. Keturah and Meli arrived at the perfect time. It was during the end of school events and D'iona and my children were excited to show their auntie all of their moves for the big dance talent show Thursday evening. We all prepared Wednesday night to attend the big dance occasion as Keturah and Meli got settled in at Zipporah's house. Everyone was exuding cheerfulness. It was now Thursday night and time for all the children to show off and present their dances with their classes. D'iona's grade was performing on this particular evening and she was a little nervous yet brave. After Amari finished his Lo Seises dance he quickly changed out of his attire. We both joined the rest of the family in the courtyard of the school. There was a large stage with an image of Saint Mary and the baby Jesus hanging in the back. The sides of the stage were sectioned off so that only the dancing classes could enter. There were five to seven rows of chairs in front of the stage. Behind those chairs were table sets and a bar. Behind the courtyard of the school were carnival rides and games. The entire school courtyard had been transformed and rearranged for this event. This was a wonderful annual event and I was happy my whole family was here to experience the laughter and smiles on the children's faces. We all watched the other performances from other classes, anxiously anticipating for D'iona's class to dance. Finally, D'iona's class was up. We all hurried to move closer to the front so we could record and cheer for our DD. The music began and those legs started moving. We frantically motioned to D'iona to smile but she ignored us and kept moving. She and the other children seemed to be having fun, still focusing hard not to make mistakes. The class's performance was amazing and D'iona did a great job because she is such a great dancer. We were all very proud. There is a private joke that DD is the greatest dancer in the family, but Amari begs to differ.

The next evening Friday was the day Amari and Aaron's class would perform. I truly enjoyed this night because it was the younger children and each class had a cute theme. Aaron's class had a *Mary Poppins* theme. They were all dressed as *Mary Poppins'* characters, ready to dance and have fun. The song selected from the movie was "A Spoonful of Sugar." It was adorable and the entire little class did great. Amari's class danced shortly afterward. They danced to "Bum Bum Tam Tam" by J. Balvin. I felt as though Amari's class did the best out of the entire school. Not to mention that Amari was the star of the show. His great dancing skills and perfect rhythm caught everyone's attention. His teacher Don Manuel seemed very happy and proud of his class's performance. There was even a mother who stopped me later that evening. She was with her husband and twin sons who were in D'iona's grade. She began to rapidly tell me in Spanish how she enjoyed watching Amari and how his dancing gave her goosebumps. I loved hearing the passion in her voice as she described Amari's dancing. I was a proud mother and aunt and was not afraid to show it. After all of the performances were complete the school immediately began cleanup and all other persons moved toward the carnival. The children were all happy and proud to have not only completed a successful year in school, but also did their best during the performances. Amos and I walked around with Aaron and Abi while Amari ventured on every ride with his best friends. We watched as the many lights blazed in our eyes, children's loud screams vibrated in our ears and the sight of the teenagers bouncing up and down on rides. This was a night to remember yet also to appreciate. There was always something special occurring for the children in this town and I was happy my children were able to encounter it.

As the school year ended many changes arose. I was becoming very attached to this small town and comfortable in this new lifestyle of pure life. Amos and I were beginning to have conversations about owning property here and settling down. I was already approaching a full year living in Spain and that made me excited. I was ready to evolve my life here and I knew it could be done. Not only was I writing a lot because I had the time now that Tina was here most mornings with Abi, but I was also absorbing the many accomplishments of my three children. They were an important reason for my writing. For instance, I can remember the day I ordered the Internet for our home. The company quickly processed my order and sent a technician to install the service. All of my children were home for the summer; therefore, not speaking Spanish as much as they were during the school year. However, something occurred this day that tickled my soul. The doorbell rang and I was greeted by two young technicians ready to do their job. I guided them in as they instantly began to search for the best place to set up the Internet device. I ushered one technician upstairs as advised and left him to work. Walking back downstairs to the other, I began to slow down as I heard Abi's little voice speaking to this man. I was completely amused and proud at the same time as I secretly listened in on a full-blown Spanish conversation between my

English speaking two-year-old daughter and the Spanish speaking Telecable technician. Both technicians were young, professional, handsome and friendly. They seemed to be in their mid-twenties to early thirties. The technician Miguel, whom Abi conversed with was a handsome man with tanned skin and dark brown hair. I noticed his nice thick beard as my husband has one as well.

"What's your name?" he asked Abi with a polite gesture and strong accent.

"ABI!" Abi aggressively responded with pride and power. I laughed to myself as I watched her hands go up.

"And how old are you?" he asked.

"Two!" Abi responded equally aggressively as she shoved her two little fingers into the air. He laughed again. I was so flabbergasted listening to my daughter speak proper Spanish to this man. I then became grateful for Tina and her lessons with Abi.

As I continued to eavesdrop, I heard the man tell Abi, "I have a little daughter like you. She's two years old too," the man stated with a kind welcome. Abi quickly placed both of her hands on each side of her cheeks with her mouth wide open in dramatic surprise. The man laughed again.

"I want to play with her!" Abi confessed in excitement.

"Well, one day if you like, you can come over to our house and play with her," Miguel proposed with a promise.

"OK," Abi maturely responded as she held her little thumb toward him in approval.

Miguel burst into laughter as he stated, "How funny!"

I peeked my head in the living room door as Miguel was laughing at this interaction with my baby girl. I could tell he was not only amazed yet he also adored Abi. He looked my way as I walked into the room.

"She speaks Spanish better than me," I jokingly confessed to him.

"Yes, but she was speaking both," he proclaimed. He was saying that Abi was essentially speaking "Spanglish." The words she did not know how to say in Spanish she interjected with English, but the man understood all. Both of my sons were there but they kept quiet and allowed Abi to have her conversation with the nice man. Finally, as the men finished their jobs at our home, Mr. Miguel said his goodbye to Abi.

"Bye, pretty girl!" he said with love.

"Bye! See you later," Abi replied as she blew kisses in the air.

Mr. Miguel chuckled again.

"How funny!" he expressed with laughter.

This tickled both Amari and me as well. All three of my children gained a great amount of the Spanish language along with the Andalusian dialogue. I suppose watching and hearing my children speak perfect Spanish with an Andalusian accent was as amusing as it would be for me to hear a small Asian child speaking English in a Southern Black American dialect.

My children were growing and so were my husband and I. Abi was learning more Spanish and becoming more mature. Aaron was making major improvements in his daily routines and experiencing fewer meltdowns. Amos was gaining more respect from his coworkers and excelling in his position. I was mastering Spanish as well as making new connections. Finally, Amari was becoming completely fluent in the language and learning his power. I would not lie and say that I did not continue my worry for his well-being while roaming the park or pool. Nonetheless, I can be honest and say that I worried less.

It was a typical late Sunday evening around seven o'clock. Outside, there were many different groups of teenagers spread throughout the outside of our community pool. The closest group to our home caught my attention because they seemed to be a little older than the average teenagers that hung around the pool in the evenings. There were about five to seven of them and their ages seemed to range from seventeen to twenty-four years. Our front door was open as the evening breeze cooled our home. The two little ones, Amos and I were all watching a movie when Amari came home from the pool. Amari's face looked slightly sad and frustrated, so I asked him what was wrong.

"Nothing," he quickly replied, but then continued. "It's just those teenagers were making fun of me," he admitted with discouragement.

"Well, what were they saying?" I asked, cringing and bracing myself for what I might hear.

"Look at the boy. Look how black he is. How black! How ugly!" Amari imitated with disgust, yet a perfect Andalusian dialect.

Both of my eyes in my head slowly rolled back as my expression was overcome with disappointment. My heart felt like a black chalkboard being slowly scratched by someone with long nails. But I had to stay calm in front of Amari.

"Where are they?" I demanded to know.

"Right there." Amari pointed.

This was the exact group of teenagers that I noticed earlier.

"OK, well I'm going over there to ask them what they had to say!" I declared in anger and pain as I headed toward the gate.

"No, Mommy! Please don't!" Amari begged me.

His small plea made me think twice.

"Yeah, Joy. They are still just kids," Amos exclaimed.

"Well, they shouldn't be speaking that way to or about a little boy," I snapped back quickly as I glanced at my shoes.

"You're right, but they are still just dumb ignorant teenagers. And you don't want the situation to escalate," Amos submitted. I thought about everything then decided to speak to my neighbor Ms. Beni. I walked outside, toward her house to see if she knew the young men. I could hear them dining out front as I rang the doorbell. Ms. Beni looked up and walked to the gate to allow me to enter.

As they sat together at the dinner table outside, I began to ask them. "Do you know those young men over there?" I pointed.

"Yes, why?" Ms. Beni answered with concern.

"Because they spoke badly about my son and I am very angry," I explained with emotion in my voice. Choking on Spanish words and phrases.

"No, no!" she exclaimed with compassion and sympathy in her eyes and voice. And she continued to rapidly explain to me in Spanish that neither my family nor I should pay attention to those young men. She elaborated to me that this group of boys was smoking and drinking. Because they are under the influence they become loud, silly and obnoxious. Ms. Beni then questioned me.

"You all are happy here in Spain, right?" she asked oratorically.

"Yes, yes," I replied with realization.

"Well, no worries, daughter!" Ms. Beni smiled at me.

I could feel my anger being subsided by the words of this beautiful wise older woman. Meanwhile, I was also fighting back tears of pain and disappointment. Essentially, what Ms. Beni wanted me to realize was that it is not important what those ignorant boys or anyone else expresses negatively about my family and me. In the end, we were all very happy here in Spain and no one could take that away from us. I was grateful for Ms. Beni and her compassion that early evening, in spite of me interrupting their *merienda* (snack or lunch). I kissed her in appreciation and went back home.

Later on, Abi became friends with Ms. Beni's granddaughter, Daniela. She was two and a half years old and her mother's name is Marta. Marta is the daughter of Ms. Beni and Mr. Luis. They were all very friendly and welcoming. Our neighbors Ms. Beni and Mr. Luis reminded me very much of my in-laws. Loving, wise, older and with a very close bond with their two grandchildren. Beni and Luis also have an adult son with a four-year-old boy, Luis III. They were always at their grandparents' house playing and spending time. I often enjoyed hearing their chinaware clicking and clattering as they dined together in the afternoon and evenings. Abi, Daniela and little Luis played great together. They enjoyed going back and forth to each other's home to play with toys. I was happy that Abi made new friends.

The summers were hot, and the air was dry. It was Amari's routine to leave for the pool every afternoon. This particular time I decided to take the two smaller ones to the pool as well. We checked in the pool at the front. Walking to an umbrella, I noticed the beautiful green grass and clear skies. It is extremely hot yet breathtaking. The pool water was clear and the children were ready to swim. I placed the arm floating tubes on Abi as we all dipped into the pool together. Holding on to Abi as she enjoys the water, I am amazed as I gaze upon my son Aaron playing in the pool. I intensely stare at him wondering what and where he was inside of his head. I watched as he repeatedly and tirelessly jumped in and out of the pool. He was having so much fun! He would hold his nose and submerge his entire body underwater. Then he would remain still for a few seconds, then do it all again. He only emerges when his lungs have no more air. I can tell that Aaron enjoys being underwater and I suspect it is the same reason that I enjoy it, because of the feeling of liberation. When the body is under the water for five to sixty seconds there is a feeling of frozen peace as all sound is muffled or muted. Nothing around is moving and you become disconnected from the world for a moment. The water seems to hold and massage his body as gravity does not apply. I continue to watch as I cradle Abi in the water. She then began to float and play with her friend Maria. This pool day not only brought my children joy but it brought Aaron peace.

Moreover, whenever we would spend the day at the local pool, we would often meet a new family. Many of the parents enjoyed the leisure of pool days because of the amazing landscaping, clear and cool water, and access to a bar. This became

Amari's favorite place to go during the summers and the bar staff seemed to adore him. One particular day, Amari was playing in the pool with all of his friends when he noticed a beautiful melanated girl who looked to be around his age. Her skin was the color of caramel and her hair was thick, black and curly. In that same moment, the girl noticed Amari too and they began to play and converse in Spanish. Her name was Isabel.

Finally, with curiosity in her eyes she asked Amari, "Are you American?"

Amari looked at her, and with his Andalusian accent, he replied, "Me? Yes! That is!"

"I am too," Isabel replied in English, exuding excitement.

Surprised and happy, Amari responded to her news by falling backward into the water to show his surprise. When he emerged Isabel was laughing in amusement. They shifted their language to English. As they talked, Amari noticed that both his friends and her friends gave Amari and Isabel the space to talk. Amari loved his friends as well as speaking Spanish. But he admitted that it was nice to have a fellow American friend that he could speak English with. Toward the end of the conversation, Isabel offered to introduce Amari to her parents. Amari obliged. Isabel first introduced Amari to her father, changing her language back to Spanish.

"Dad. This is my new friend, Amari. He's American and from Florida," Isabel politely stated.

"Nice to meet you," Isabel's father calmly responded.

"Same to you," Amari responded with a curious look on his face.

Amari could hear a difference in the accent of Isabel's father. He could not resist his urge to ask.

"Wait. You're American too?" Amari asked with wonder.

Isabel's father politely chuckled and said, "Yes, but I'm Colombian American."

Amari smiled with understanding and just replied maturely with a simple OK.

"Wait! You're American and from Florida?" Isabel's mother interjected. She was a beautiful Black American woman with long black wavy hair. Her American accent was proper and refreshing to Amari.

"Yes, I am," Amari answered.

"I would have guessed that you were from New York or somewhere else besides Florida!" Isabel's mother confessed.

Amari smiled as Isabel's parents invited him to have lunch with them. He accepted with confidence, knowing Amos and I would not object. Isabel also had an adorable five-year-old little brother and he was very well-spoken. As the afternoon continued with Isabel's family, they ate, continue to make acquaintances, then they played a popular Spanish board game by the name of La Oca. Isabel's father kept winning. Afterward, Amari and Isabel went back to the pool for a little longer. As the night came to an end, Isabel's parents told Amari that it was nice meeting him and they hoped to meet his parents soon. Amari became friends with an entire family and that made me glow inside. For the remainder of that summer Amari and Isabel played together at the pool whenever they saw each other. He even found out that she would be attending Salesianos the following school year. Moreover, until this day, we had never met this family. Nevertheless, I had the spiritual speculation that many people Amari met throughout the summer were only meant for him to meet. I believed God was giving Amari ways to learn and be encouraged. Reminding him that he will never be alone no matter the country he is in.

Two friends in particular that have remained constant are Joséchu and Bosco. Joséchu is a little boy who befriended Amari at the pool one summer. From that day forward, Amari and little Joséchu became inseparable. So inseparable that Amari became a part of his family. Joséchu was only four years old and Amari eight when they first met. But Amari's outgoing personality and rapid fluent Spanish caused locals to be very comfortable around him. Little Joséchu became like Amari's Spanish little brother. He is absolutely gorgeous with tanned skin, blue eyes and thick brown wavy hair. His father, Joséchu, has a stern disposition but a fun and kind personality. He is the founder and owner of a French learning academy here in Utrera. His wife, Inma, is extremely sweet with an astounding and unique beauty that she passed on to both their children, little Joséchu and Maria. Maria (ten years old at the time) was also one of Abi's first friends that she made from the pool. I could tell that Maria adored Abi and always played with her whenever they saw each other. Amari and Joséchu played so well together that the entire family grew to adore him. He became like an additional member of their family. They played at the pool, his house, went to soccer games and other family outings. For instance, there was a time when Amari was out with Joséchu and his family. They went to a local soccer game here in Utrera. After the game, Amari and little Joséchu were able to meet some of the soccer players. After hearing Amari's Spanish, one of the soccer players mentioned that he was surprised to find out Amari is American. He assumed that Amari was an adopted child. There was an additional incident when Amari was out to dinner with little Joséchu and his family. Amari was approached by a beautiful middle-aged African woman. She carried a large basket with fresh fruit on top of her head.

"Hello," she said to him in French.

"Hello," Amari responded in French.

"So, you speak French?" the African woman asked, now curious.

"Yes, well I'm learning it in school," Amari answered.

"Where are you from?" Her interest grew.

"The United States," Amari responded.

"Oh, so you're American!" the African woman loudly exclaimed in English.

"Yes, ma'am," Amari politely answered switching to English with her.

"Well, your French is very good!" she complimented Amari.

"Thank you," Amari said.

"You are a very educated young boy," the woman admitted to Amari with pride.

"Thank you," Amari repeated, still smiling.

They waved goodbye to each other and she walked away. Meanwhile, little Joséchu and his family silently listened. After the beautiful African woman walked away, Big Joséchu had to know:

"Amari, does that happen to you often?" Joséchu asked as Inma looked on.

"Not often, but sometimes," Amari simply responded.

Joséchu was fluent in French and understood their entire conversation. He was even surprised to hear Amari speak French so well. I quickly realized that Amari has the gift of language and that we needed to cultivate it.

This exact same scenario went for Bosco. Bosco is also younger than Amari. He is a little blonde boy with dark brown eyes. He seemed slightly timid but not with Amari. They had a beautiful bond and friendship. Bosco's mother's name is Lola. She is beautiful, sweet and intelligent. She was very easy to talk to and provided a lot of clarity for me whenever I had questions. She is a native Spanish and English-speaking psychologist in Seville. Little Bosco's father, Big Bosco, is an engineer. They also have a beautiful adolescent daughter named Gloria. Bosco's family often came to pick Amari up to accompany them on their various family activities. I believe his ability to speak their language so perfectly made him even more charming than he already is. It proved to me how important it can be to learn a different language. The natives respected him for learning and us for trying. I was so grateful that Amari had two sound families that he could all call his true friends. Their relationship with my son is extremely authentic and unwavering.

We were all becoming more integrated into the culture of Spain, as we also became accustomed to the ways of this small town. However, a common issue that we have had here in Spain is people touching our hair. Especially my children. I understand that there are not many people of color in Utrera, Spain. I also realize that our skin and hair may seem exotic to the locals.

However, I cannot avoid my culture and who I am. I do not prefer my children's hair being touched, or mine. In Black American culture, our hair is considered sacred; therefore, it is considered rude for others to touch it. I love that most strangers are extremely friendly and welcoming to my family and me. Yet, I strongly dislike some of their thought processes. Many people are ignorant and feel they have the right to put their hands into my children's hair without permission. We even had to teach our children to politely ask people not to touch their hair in Spanish. For example, this summer, Amari came home complaining about how his companions would not stop touching his hair. I asked him if he asked them to stop and explained his culture. Amari assured me that he did explain, but they kept touching his hair anyway. Hearing this made me very angry. Amos and I explained to Amari that if someone is touching him without his consent then at that point it is physical harassment. Thus, Amari should physically defend himself. I wanted this to be his last option; therefore, I thought it would be best for Tia Patri (Tina's mother) and me to speak with the pool staff about this issue.

One night, as I sat outside enjoying the night breeze, I could hear a scooter rushing along the sidewalk about one hundred to two hundred feet away. I immediately knew that it was Amari. I searched his face for any indication of trouble as I unlocked the gate for him. I could tell that he was upset but he surprisingly hid it very well. After a little prying, I finally got Amari to tell me what happened: There was a group of older teenagers that befriended Amari at the park, next to the pool. They continuously touched Amari's hair. Amari politely explained his culture and asked them repeatedly not to touch his hair. But they continued to touch it against his will. Not only were they touching his hair, but they were also pulling it out and hurting him. This caused Amari to explode with anger. Amari suddenly kneeled on one knee to punch one boy while simultaneously elbowing another boy in his stomach as hard as he could. Both teenagers bent over in pain then ran away. The rest of his friends seemed frightened by Amari's sudden anger and followed their friend as they all ran away like cowards.

"The next time you touch my hair I'll break your arm!" Amari shouted at them with a fierce Andalusian accent.

We do not condone violence or anger. But, in this incident I was proud of Amari for channeling his anger and using it to protect himself.

After multiple incidences of Amari having to defend himself with people touching his hair, I had grown worried. Amari was spending all of his days at the pool and I wanted to ensure my son was safe. On a day that I was stressed with the agony of Amari being bullied, he came home boasting about a new friend he made from South Africa named Mpho. While Amari was playing at the pool, he noticed a melanated teenager with his group of friends. Mpho and Amari introduced themselves and began to talk. They began their conversation in Spanish yet ended it in English once Mpho realized Amari is an American. Though he was a bit surprised, the teenager admitted that he thought Amari was African. As they continued to converse, Amari noticed that Mpho started to touch his hair.

However, he seemed hesitant to touch Amari's hair. This made Amari think. "Do you have problems with people touching your hair too?" Amari asked lightly while playing in his own hair.

Mpho slowly yet passionately nodded. "Yes, always."

Amari saw a great opportunity to gain advice from this older black boy.

"So how do you get them to stop?" Amari continued, eager for an answer.

"I knock them out," Mpho responded with a serious smirk on his face.

"How?" Amari's questions continued.

"I use this special move," Mpho stated as he demonstrated.

He swiftly bent down, kneeling on one knee. His arms and clenched fists precisely came straight out, appearing to be punching someone in the stomach.

Amari liked his move and immediately tried to replicate it. As he looked back at Mpho, Mpho put both his thumbs up in approval. Both he and Amari continued to converse as they practiced the move repeatedly until Amari mastered it. Mpho even introduced Amari to his entire family. His mother, father and little five-year-old cousin. Amari stated that the family was extremely nice to him. Once again, Amari had made friends with an entire family all by himself. This encounter was like a divine blessing for Amari. He has been having problems with local children touching his hair against his will, harassing him. Then out of nowhere, he essentially meets an older version of himself wherein he could receive guidance. I felt as though God used

Mpho's presence, once again to remind Amari that he was not alone. Amari and Mpho became good friends.

One day, as Amari was coming home from the pool, he noticed a scuffle. He realized it was Mpho being attacked by two other teenagers! They were both pulling Mpho's hair. Without thinking, Amari dashed toward Mpho and tackled one of the teenagers. The boy then ran away leaving his friend. Without any fear Amari proceeded to help Mpho with the other teenager. However, this other boy was not giving up very easily. The boy grabbed Amari's hair with force. He chuckled and scuffled with both Amari and Mpho. He thought it was a game. Amari grabbed the boy from behind, allowing Mpho to punch the boy. The boy broke free and ran in an attempt to escape. But still angry, Mpho pursued him. He caught the boy and body slammed him in slow motion. The boy cried out in pain and defeat as he finally gave up.

"Don't touch my hair, bitch!" Mpho angrily shouted in Spanish at the teenager as he ran away.

Amari looked on in pride. Mpho then turned to Amari and dapped him up.

"Thanks for helping me, Amari," Mpho stated in gratitude.

"Of course," Amari responded with Spanish slang.

As stated before, Amos and I do not condone violence. Nonetheless, I equally encourage Amari to pick and choose his battles wisely. In my discernment, I viewed Amari and his new friend Mpho as reflections of one another; that they needed each other. Although I am not always around my children, God's protection will never leave them. God has sent great teachers, a safe environment, many valuable lessons, but most importantly love to my children while here in Spain. For that I will rejoice. For God says in his Word: "Rejoice in the Lord always, and again I say, Rejoice. Let your moderation be known to all men. For the Lord is at hand. Be careful for nothing; but in everything by prayer, supplication, and thanksgiving let your request be known unto God. And the peace of God which passed all understanding, shall keep your hearts and minds through Christ Jesus" (Philippians 4:4–7).

Chapter 3:

Harmonious Bonds

Not only were my children making good and friendly connections here in town, but I was as well. I have always been a woman of pride and privacy, yet I would always develop beautiful relationships wherever I would go, and Spain was no different. I seemed to be tapping more into my spiritual gifts and also becoming more of myself within these past years. Moving to Spain has escalated these spiritual evolvements and caused me to ponder on how my family and I could utilize our gifts and talents. I knew my family's worth, and that we had much to learn but also much to teach.

During the first few weeks of the boys attending school, I began to meet the parents of their classmates. These daily interactions with some of the mothers soon became friendships. The first mother I met and became close to was Vanessa. Vanessa personally introduced herself to me and stated that her daughter, Maria, was in Amari's class. She explained that she was a "Spanish military brat," which is an American term used to describe a child or young adult who has been raised in a military home. Vanessa was welcoming and she made me feel comfortable. Not to mention that she too, was certified in English. Thus, her English speaking and comprehension were very good. Her family and ours quickly became close friends as we all began to spend time together. Vanessa and her husband, José, reminded me of friends from "the block"; in other words, they felt very familiar to me and I cherished our family bond. Vanessa introduced me to many other mothers; she showed me around the town and made it her duty to ensure I became acquainted with the Utrera way. I was greatly appreciative of Vanessa and her entire family. Not only did we become close, but she and Zipporah established an immediate connection as well. They both possessed a silly humor and a slightly wild side. One day Vanessa and I agreed to meet in front of the school to take the children to a park in the plaza. Vanessa informed me that this park was very popular in town and many of the parents would have drinks at the bars and restaurants while the children would run freely around and play. On this particular day is when Zipporah and Vanessa met. They clicked instantly.

Zipporah was a little apprehensive about her move here as I stated before. She felt the town lacked diversity and that posed a problem for her. Nevertheless, that was the same day we all met Fatou, our African friend from Senegal. As the children played and became familiar with one another we women all talked and laughed. Zipporah and Fatou exchanged numbers as we made plans to stay connected. I was happy to make a new friend of color who possessed knowledge of Utrera and Spain. Fatou was also helpful throughout the year and she became like our own blood sister. One morning after dropping the children to school, Zipporah, Fatou and I met for pastries and coffee. This was a common thing to do in the mornings. As we shared our life stories and became more acquainted, my mind began to wonder. I wanted to know Fatou's perspective on living in Spain as a traditional African woman from Senegal. It was interesting to hear her elaboration and explanation of living in Spain. She explained to me and Zipporah about the people, their culture and their lack of knowledge of the African people. While listening and comprehending I drew my own conclusions. In my personal perception, "Africanos" are treated a little differently here in Spain than us Black Americans. It almost seems as though the majority of Spaniards are a little prejudiced against African people. I was even reminded of the instance when Amari was visiting the camp house of one of his friends and the great-aunt ignorantly asked Amari about our family:

"Well, if y'all are not rich Americans then are y'all poor Africans?"

I was appalled that Amari had to be exposed to such ignorance by adults and wanted to confront this nosy and rude woman.

This miseducated perception is similar to the way Mexicans are viewed in America. Many Mexicans are in America illegally. Because of their illegal status in the country, it may create a domino effect on the overall economy. However, many Mexicans are normal US citizens and successful Americans just like the rest. Nevertheless, they are sometimes treated with disrespect because they come to America to make better lives for themselves. Therefore, they may take jobs from the hands of other Americans. Yet these jobs they accept are often low paying, harsh and unjust. Many Americans complain, like many Spaniards complain, that these jobs are for the citizens. Nonetheless, Fatou exclaimed that many Africans come to Spain to flee from the corruption of their own government and to build a better life. They do not desire to live among a culture and people that are not of their own, but sometimes people are forced to make decisions for the betterment of their children. This same scenario and truth apply to the Mexicans in America. In the end, I have come to the conclusion that Spaniards are very protective of their country and as long as you come to contribute to their economy and not take from it, they are somewhat willing to accept but with discretion. This I have learned to respect and comment less upon because it can be a sensitive subject to broach. I will never fully understand the ways or some of the people here, yet I can find my own understanding through friendships, pure love, and my desire to learn.

Fatou's children were not students of Salesianos, but I made it my purpose to connect our children. I felt it was important for my children to maintain relationships with children of all races, cultures and beliefs. This would surely broaden their horizon. Many of the parents from my children's school are Catholic. However, Fatou was a Pentecostal Christian like myself and this developed a closer bond between us.

As the year rapidly continued I too continued to associate myself more with the other mothers. I soon met most of Amari's closest friend's parents and I grew to love some of them. Natalia, the mother of Greta and a Spanish military spouse was one of those parents I loved. Greta and Amari became very close in school. They were like best friends and wanted that to be known. It was a must for myself and Amos to meet her parents. As I became more acquainted with Natalia, I learned that she is a psychiatrist. She is a wonderful person and incredibly sweet. She was one of the first mothers who introduced herself to me and added me to the WhatsApp group for the class. She did not speak much English, but her comprehension was very strong. She later explained to me that she reads a lot of paperwork in English at her job and that's how she understands more than she speaks. The moment that I felt a connection between Natalia and me was when she shared with me that she too is a military spouse and knew how it felt to pick up and start all over again. That meant a lot to me. Natalia is beautiful, kind, gentle, intelligent, and a great mother and wife.

Through Natalia is how I met one of her best friends, Emilia. Emilia is the mother of Iván Luis, one of the first friends that Amari made as they then quickly became best friends. When the mothers first added me to their WhatsApp group, I sent a personal separate message to Emilia because I wanted to meet the mother of Iván Luis. I wanted to know who was raising this sweet boy who befriended my son in spite of their cultural differences. Emilia and I soon exchanged a sweet dialogue. Our first time interacting, Emilia quickly informed me that she knew zero English. To make it easier for us to communicate, I used the translator. We both laughed about how our boys constantly spoke of one another at home. Amari's teacher, Don Manuel, even informed Emilia of their rapidly growing friendship. She and I both agreed that we were very happy about our boy's friendship with one another. I told her that I was learning Spanish. I elaborated on the struggle with the Spanish grammar and words that all sound the same. Emilia quickly encouraged me that through patience and time I would learn the language. "Little by little," she would say to me. I instantly felt a beautiful connection with this mother from that small exchange. She let me know that she was willing to assist me in any way that I needed. Emilia is a beautiful petite woman who dressed very stylishly, which was not uncommon in southern Spain. She was kind, bold and fun! She also has a beautiful younger daughter named Cayetana who is so cute. Her husband's name is Agustín and he is also a nice person.

As my bonds increased, my interactions did as well. I was now a part of a group of women who not only respected me, but they respected each other. As I observed these mothers, I could see their flaws and strengths, as they could mine. However, they seemed to mesh very well together. One morning as I was attempting to return home from walking the children to school, I was approached by a beautiful mother who introduced herself as Conso A., short for Consolación. Conso A. and I exchanged numbers, as well as friendly conversation. I stored her contact information in my phone, labeling it as Conso A. This name was very common within the Sevilla province. It was interesting yet puzzling to know various women with the same name. With my curiosity, I asked Conso why so many women shared the same name. She was proud to share with me the history of the name *La Virgen de Consolación*; this is the name of the patroness of Utrera. Conso informed me that each town and city in Spain have a patron saint or the Virgin Mary. They believe that the spirit of the patron or Saint Mary protects their town or city. How intriguing! I soon realized that Conso A. was the mother of Alejandro, another classmate and friend of Amari's. I could see that Conso is a good mother to her two boys. She was married to her husband, Antonio, and at times I felt she desired more gratitude from her husband and boys. I believe Conso A. is powerful in her own right and possesses the potential to be a savvy businesswoman. My connection with Conso A was deeper than the other mothers because we both share common personality traits. She is fun, easy to talk to, kind, strong, honest and courageous. Courageous because she admitted that my sister and I inspired her to take English classes at the local school in town. As we continued to socialize, she began to explain to me that she lives near many Americans and wants to extend herself to them. Conso A. also possesses wisdom beyond her years and was happy to impart that wisdom with me whenever we spoke. With that wisdom Conso A. stated to me one morning, "You cannot learn with fear," in her strong Utrera accent. I took those words with me whenever I would attempt to speak to others in Spanish. The less I became afraid or ashamed, the more I spoke with confidence. Conso A. was right. Over the course of time, I felt like Antonio Banderas from the movie *The 13th Warrior*, during the scene when Antonio was captured and sitting at a campfire with his captors. Over the course of my two years of living here, I began to recognize small words, the small words turned into small phrases. The phrases turned into full sentences and the progression continued. My Spanish speaking still needs a lot of work, but I understand about 70 percent. Conso A. then invited me to breakfast with her and other mothers from the school. That one invite transposed into a morning routine for me. I was becoming more a part of this town and loving every moment.

As the fall approached and the winter holidays began to decrease, I noticed my time decreasing as well. I could clearly see that living in a small town could sometimes be more strenuous than living in a large city. However, it was a change I was fortunate to adapt to.

My day would consist of nonstop movement, from taking the children to school to breakfast with the ladies to errands for the house. My weeks became days, hours became minutes, and minutes seconds. There were many new changes I was becoming accustomed to. For instance, birthday parties for the children. In the United States I can remember taking Amari to birthday parties hosted in the backyard, or at a local theme park in town. The parents would drop the children off at the party with the option of staying to assist or leaving for the afternoon. These birthday parties were not often, and not every child was fortunate to have one. However, in Utrera many children would have a birthday party, usually hosted at the same locations in town. I can recall Aaron being invited to one of his classmate's birthday parties and he had a blast. Amari was then invited to a party and he was thrilled about it. The party was for Maria, Vanessa's daughter, and she, Amari and D'iona played very well together. When Vanessa invited us, I was both excited and appreciative. Before arriving, Vanessa was kind enough to explain to me in English how birthday parties were done here in the local area. She explained that each parent of the child invited to the party, would give five euros to the mother hostess. The host parents of the event would then use the money to purchase one large gift for the child. This concept was so simple, fair and organized in my opinion. I loved it!

We dropped Amari, D'iona and Aaron off at Illusionland, which is a very popular location for children's birthday parties here in Utrera. The mothers would then meet for drinks at a bar nearby to socialize and catch up. There were only a few mothers accompanying me and Zipporah as well as little Abi. Nonetheless, I really enjoyed the time with these few mothers because I was able to receive revelations about the Spanish language. In her past, Vanessa studied English for years and she was very confident in speaking it. However, a few other mothers at the table knew a little English as well, yet they preferred not to speak it. In my conclusion, I believe they lacked the desire to speak English the same way I lacked the desire to speak Spanish. It was the fear and nervousness to sound silly or be incorrect. This observation made me realize that if I was serious about learning Spanish, it was a must for me to move past my insecurity of sounding silly or incorrect. I would need to speak the language anyway. This birthday party was the first of many that our children attended together throughout the school year. I loved how we the parents would often encounter the opportunity to practice our Spanish, exchange cultures, and get to know each other better. I am sure I was not the only parent feeling appreciation for these meets and greets.

Over the course of the next few months, my family and I began to make many new friends and acquaintances. Many of them opening up their homes and lives to us for which we were very grateful. It was at these many events that my family and I were able to learn and expand our knowledge of the Spanish culture. From their language to their way of living, our friends here in Utrera were happy and proud to share their customs and traditions with us. As I reminisce on these customs and traditions, I think of the love they have for family, close friendships and the children. The people of Utrera loved to party together, whether strangers or friends. However, when the friends got together it would be a wild and exciting night. For Amos and me, we first experienced a wild episode with friends when we were invited to a BBQ. The family BBQ was hosted by Natalia and her husband José, and they were thrilled that we obliged. I could sense that they were proud to show us the military park there in Utrera.

We arrived at the barbecue, which was located on the outskirts of Utrera. The park was beautiful! It was private and could only be accessed by Spanish military members and their families or friends. José, Natalia's husband, was our access as he was not hesitant to show us around the area. The park had multiple fields, hills, grills, and so forth. There were four families that attended the BBQ and we all integrated very well together. First there was the host family, Natalia and José and their daughter Greta. Then there were their closest friends Emilia and Augustin, along with their son Iván Luis and younger daughter Cayetana. Also, Maria and Fernando who were new friends of ours and they have two beautiful twin girls around Aaron's age. This was actually Maria and Fernando's first time meeting José and Natalia. Nevertheless, we all connected with ease. This was also one of the days that I truly learned how Spaniards party. They are very organized and calculating when planning gatherings. I learned that they focus on family, community, love, and fairness as we would all split the costs of the food and drinks. We would sometimes shop together or cook for one another. At every event I noticed they made sure to have plenty of beers and enough liquor. One liquor I noticed at most events was Utrera's signature drink, Anís. As we all drank, danced and laughed, it was mandatory for Amos and me to be introduced to the "rules of a Spanish party." The first rule of a Spanish party is to never have an empty hand. Either a beer or drink must always be in your hand throughout the entire time. The second rule is that you must be willing to party all day and night. We started the barbecue at around four o'clock in the afternoon and did not leave until around midnight. We all had a beautiful and great time! We ate, laughed, danced, drank and got to know one another more personally. The children equally enjoyed themselves. They played and danced all day and night! They wanted to hear some of our favorite songs. I showed Emilia and Natalia how to twerk while our husbands laughed at the sight. It was hilarious watching these European women stiffly move their bodies to imitate the "twerking" dance. I laughed until my abs ached as we danced with drinks in our hands. I began to feel sleepy toward the end of the barbecue and quickly dozed off in my chair. I can remember how José made fun of me. He made me feel so embarrassed for falling asleep, yet he was kind and humorous. How dare I fall asleep during a Spanish party? ¡No bueno! Which leads to the third rule. Never sleep during a party!

As Maria and I continued to converse after I was clowned for sleeping, I realized that she is a great person. She is beautiful, kind, a great mother and a great wife. She is also smart and outspoken. I would describe Maria and her husband as "conservative free spirits." Maria and I became very close friends. I felt very comfortable with her. She helped me with my Spanish as she would always speak both Spanish and English when we conversed. This tactic of hers would assist me in continuously learning. She became the type of friend that was always there when I needed her. Her husband, Fernando, is a registered nurse. He is a kindhearted person and together they make a beautiful couple. His English is not bad, and I could tell that he and his wife were excited to reengage their English. Whenever we met up with Fernando and Maria, we were usually accompanied by Emilia and Augustin. Sometimes Natalia and José would join us when they had the time. We always ended up having the greatest times! Laughing, drinking, dancing, eating and singing. Fernando and Emilia were always the two lives of the party singing, joking and making us laugh so hard that we could barely breathe. I loved Fernando's energy, great sense of style, humor, intelligence and willingness to teach.

Emilia's husband, Agustin, possessed a great sense of humor as well. Augo is what his close friends and family call him. He is kind, calm and humorous.

José, the husband of Natalia, was a little different from the other fathers. In my opinion he had more in common with my husband. He is very easy to talk to. He is a firefighter from the Spanish military, and he and Natalia have been living in Utrera for the past few years. José is handsome, kind, intelligent and funny. He is a man of honor and proud to serve his country. When we first met at the gate for the BBQ, I immediately knew he had a good spirit. José seemed to take the lead on the barbecue because his English was the best of the group. He always challenged me to speak *only* Spanish when we conversed. José gave me the best piece of advice when it came to learning a different language. He advised me that with each new word I learn, I must find a way to continuously use it until that word is embedded into my Spanish vocabulary. He counseled me to not just memorize a new word, but use it in my everyday life in order to let it sink in. I took his advice and it has tremendously helped me in my Spanish learning journey.

In my observation of this group of friends I first noticed the life of Natalia. For example, she is a very prideful woman, and she honors her profession. I remembered being once like her. Overworked, minimum time with my husband due to military obligations, and the forced pressure of having to sometimes play the "single mother" role. One day, I simply felt her energy in my spirit, and I knew exactly what she was going through. Her pride and sense of privacy kept her from reaching out for any help. I used the voice of God and the gift that he gave me to reach out to her and be brash about what I felt from her. I feel as though she received it, but only in that moment. All I could do was be obedient and know that what I speak will always be in love and understanding. This has always been common for me for most of my life. Whenever my spirit would command me to speak I would. Some would receive my advisement and others would not. I could also appreciate the friends that advised me as well. There was much more for me to learn.

Utrera possessed a lively atmosphere and many hidden jewels. I can recall when Tia Patri, Tina's mother, told me about a large market in town that occurred every Wednesday from ten in the morning until two. There were many things I needed, and she assured me this was the best place to go. Tia Patria asked if I wanted to join her at the market this particular Wednesday. I was happy to accept her invitation and get Abi out of the house. This market had everything from clothes to shoes to fabrics, fruits and more. During my time at the market with Tia Patri and Abi, I met a new friend. After completing our last-minute shopping, we went to one of the food trucks for lunch. As we stood in line to order, a beautiful melanated woman with a shiny, black curly Afro and glasses caught my attention. She had a beautiful daughter who looked to be Abi's age and I could tell that she was biracial. We made eye contact and smiled at each other. I took this gesture as an invitation to approach her. I left my line to approach this woman in her line.

"Hola," I said with a friendly smile

"Hola," she responded, matching my smile. Her Spanish had a different dialect, which intrigued me more. We then introduced ourselves with the traditional Spanish kiss. She shared with me that she was originally from the Dominican Republic. Consequently, her Spanish accent was a little different. However, growing up in South Florida, I was familiar with the Latino Spanish and that thought made me feel at home. I spoke to her using the little Spanish that I knew, as Tia Patri approached us later to help us communicate. In the end, we exchanged numbers and began communicating.

Our families finally met at her daughter Claudia's birthday party a few months later. Over the course of time, Maria, Zipporah and I became very close. She became our sister. And her husband, Danny, and daughter, Claudia, became our brother and niece. We all absolutely loved each other's company. And I loved having a melanated friend that spoke fluent Spanish. I view Maria as a powerful, beautiful, funny, vibrant and charismatic queen. She is also a talented seamstress and designer. When I discovered her profession, I quickly booked her to design my family's and my flamenco attire for the annual feria this year. Her husband, Danny, is from northern Albacete, Spain. He was a schoolteacher at one of the public schools in Utrera. Danny is handsome, smart and honest. His English is at an intermediate level due to his time spent in the United States. Danny, for me, was a kindred spirit and I felt very comfortable around him.

Later on, Danny fell into a short deep depression over his health. He had a stomach condition that restricted his diet. This caused him to be sick and weak. He was finally diagnosed and getting better. All we could do was offer our support and be there for them. However, we all had faith and prayed for his speedy recovery. This posed a struggle for Maria at times for she loved her husband and wanted him better again. She would be home most of the time with their daughter, Claudia, ensuring her husband had time to rest. Claudia was energetic, stubborn and adorable. She was a free-spirit baby and she and Abi played well together. Maria and I continued to make the effort to meet up and converse for each other and for our children. She and Zipporah became close as well, laughing, dancing and interacting like two young girls in grade school. It was always fun to watch them together. After about six months of Danny struggling with his health, Maria and he made a decision to move back to his hometown. They needed time for Danny to recover mentally, physically and financially. I supported their plan, but Zipporah and I were sad to see our sister leave. This was only temporary, and I prayed God would send them back to Seville.

    The summer was rapidly approaching, and I was ready for my first full summer, being that I arrived in Spain at the end of the last one. One of my favorite happenings within the approaching summer was receiving news that Maria and her family would be moving back to Seville. After about eight months of not seeing my dear friend, I was ready to have her and her family back into the routine of my life. On this particular day my cousin Nene was in town and we were returning from a stroll through the town. Danny called Zipporah earlier that day to address his desire to see all of us before he returned home. Zipporah offered him a room to rest in her house so that he wouldn't need to drive back to Seville after visiting with the family. Zipporah texted me that evening to let me know Danny was at our house, that he was looking to spend time and give some good news. Nene, Amari and I hurried home to greet our guest. When we arrived home, Amos, Zipporah and Danny were all sitting outside talking. I was happy to see him because we all really missed them. He updated me on their lives. Maria and Claudia were both doing great. Claudia was learning and speaking more, and Maria was working on her body goals and succeeding. Danny's health was significantly improving, and I could tell from looking at him. However, Maria was unhappy with her employment and having a hard time adapting to the town. Nonetheless, Danny was blessed to receive a teaching position in Dos Hermanas, a small town fifteen minutes north of Utrera.

This meant they would be returning back to Andalusia within four to six months. I jumped up dancing in excitement. We all laughed, and Danny shared with us the spiritual significance of his job location. *Dos hermanas* translates in English as "two sisters." Zipporah and I looked at each other in amazement because Danny was referring to us as being Maria's dos hermanas—a beautiful revelation symbolizing that our families still had a lot to learn from each other.

Before the summer arrived, I can recollect the entire winter as each moment raced through my mind. The winter is usually my worst season and I often dread the months spent in the cold. However, living in Spain has changed my perspective on winters. I now live in a town where celebrations are often throughout the year, and during the holidays the town becomes like a grand fair, with decorative Christmas lights on every street. There was always a party we were invited to and we did our best to attend all. For instance, there was a large gathering hosted at the bowling alley involving three large families in one place. We all wanted to connect as a group and bring the children together during the holidays. There were Vanessa, José and their three girls; Stella and her son Pelayo; Conso A., her husband Antonio and their two boys; and of course, Amos and me with our three children. Once we arrived at the event, I could see everyone sitting in the back at a large table. Laughter, joy, and the sound of pins shattering filled the room. Amari quickly joined his friends at a bowling lane as they began a new game. Aaron joined him as Abi stayed by my side. Zipporah and I sat with the other ladies and ordered drinks. Amos joined the other fathers for a bowling game, same as the children. It was fun watching them compete and have fun, cracking jokes and sipping drinks. Our kids remained playing and laughing the entire night. We ladies laughed, danced, talked and drank, as I listened to Conso A. explaining our dance class to them all. Her words dripped with passion as she spoke about her experience in the class. I enjoyed listening to them talking to one another, as I took in every moment, enjoying the sound of their accents.

Amos was now talking with the other husbands at the bar. Zipporah was conversing with a group of young adults two tables down. As I sat at the table with the mothers, I took notes on my observations of everyone in the room. Suddenly everyone began to make their way to the bar for a toast. We all toasted to friendship.

I began to converse with Vanessa and her husband José. Our conversation shifted to their beautiful love story, that they were willing to share with me. Vanessa lived in the United States of America from the year 2005 until the year 2008 to study English. Living over four thousand miles from her country, family and home were extremely hard for Vanessa. She was depressed, homesick, not eating but too prideful to admit it to her family. So, Vanessa called on someone she knew that she could trust emotionally. Her friend José. He came to visit her two months in the beginning and two months at the end of her stay in America. Jose's visits meant a lot to Vanessa because he was her only support system at the time. But José admitted that he was already madly in love with Vanessa before he visited her. He confessed that he came to her because he wanted to admit his love to her. Vanessa was happy to hear this news for she was feeling the same. They got married in 2009 and have been inseparable ever since.

Vanessa and José have a beautiful relationship and marriage. They seem to balance each other perfectly. However, after nine-plus years of marriage and three children later, Vanessa has changed. Every mother knows how our bodies permanently change once we have children. This is a common struggle with women who have had children and I also have struggled with the same insecurities. Even though Vanessa is so beautiful on the inside and out; she may not always see it in herself. Additionally, Vanessa and José are schoolteachers with three children and busy schedules. I feel that Vanessa enjoys teaching, but many times she may have felt as though she was missing out on a lot because of her busy schedule. This, in my opinion, added to her insecurities. I noticed this same issue with a few Spanish mothers who are employed. Many of them work because they want to feel productive. They may or may not work because they have financial obligations. Some women feel that being a stay-at-home mother is simply not enough. I can reminisce on the times I felt the same. I wanted more so I started classes at a local community college. I then quickly realized my worth as a mother and that school was not for me; that being a mother was more than enough. I came to the conclusion that much of my stress came from me and the way I allowed my children to depend on me too heavily. I notice this same issue here in Utrera. Living in a small town has helped me to discover my need to get away and let loose, yet many times I can get away responsibly with my children with me. Most of the mothers here have mastered this way of living.

My family and I finally left the building but noticed that Zipporah was missing. The bowling alley was only less than a mile from our homes. After Amos and I bathed and tucked the children into bed, I walked back to check on Zipporah to ensure she was fine. I found her inside of the bowling alley at the bar with some of our friends. Finally, Zipporah, Conso A., her husband, Antonio, Stella and I all went off on a small drunken tangent, talking loud about nothing. Zipporah somehow convinced Conso onto her back, tipsy and unaware of Conso's weight. As Conso attempted to climb on, they both tumbled to the ground in weakness. Stella and I were bent over in hysterical laughter. I felt the need to take charge and helped Conso into her car. She waved goodbye to us all as they drove off. Zipporah and I gave kisses to the others who stayed and made our way back to the house nearby. Walking and talking about the night, we both divulged that our time here in Spain has been healing our mindset of the European people. Our true connections in Spain help perpetuate this growth. Zipporah and I are both grateful for this mental and spiritual transition.

The next day there was another event planned for the evening. We all felt it would be nice to dine together outside of dance class. Meanwhile, this was also a tradition they celebrated as friends annually, to have a big brunch together. Zipporah and I were honored to not only be leaders of this class, but friends they chose to invite. The brunch started at two thirty; however, Zipporah and I arrived fashionably late. When we walked in, dressed to impress, the ladies all greeted us with admiration and love. Looking around I noticed the elegance of this restaurant and how crowded it was. Every woman at our table was adorned in a fine dress or top. Their faces were painted to perfection, and hair freshly styled. This was such a beautiful experience. Both my sister and I felt absolutely privileged to have been welcomed into this dynamic group of friends. It was extremely loud inside of the restaurant as though the strumming of a large bass is thumping through my body. The sounds of many conversations, laughter, plates and glasses clashing all surround me like an aura of happiness. Our Spanish is still very limited, but I suspect the women somewhat enjoy using the translator. The constant passing of cellphones back and forth; each party hoping that it has the correct translation. It is sort of comical. Zipporah was soaking in the experience as well. She has even gotten a little emotional while basking in the moment. These women are so accommodating. They honor my sister's "conscious eating" lifestyle and make sure that she has a clear understanding of the menu. Consequently, the cross-culturalization continues. Some of these women from the group have remained acquaintances, and others have become my dearest friends. Sitting on my right was Stella. She is the life of the group and very fun! Most of the time Stella is silly and goofy, yet she does not care what others think. She is sweet, talkative and very special. She has a very big personality and I adore her sociable spirit. As I mentioned before, Stella is the mother of Amari's classmate and friend Pelayo. To be honest, when I first met Stella, I was not sure if we would connect well. I can be very conservative and private. That causes me to talk or share less. Stella is very open and outgoing, and I was not sure if we would mesh. However, I was wrong and over time, we became very close. She, along with most of my Spanish friends, has been instrumental in my Spanish learning. She had the desire to improve her English and I had the desire to learn Spanish. We both helped each other achieve that goal. Stella practiced her English with me, and I practiced my Spanish with her. I cannot quite explain the feeling, but I always felt as if I were in a movie scene whenever I spent time with Stella. She would always speak her native tongue with passion and deep feeling, while, I spoke my native tongue with confidence and pride. I preferred her to speak to me in her tongue, but I also understood that she desired to learn as much as I did. As time progressed, Stella became one of my favorite people.

Sitting vertically across from me was Johnnie, a bright, fun, crazy young mother from Utrera. She is married with two sons. She always had a smile on her face. I really like Johnnie because she is full of love and happiness. Sometimes Johnnie would be in a confrontation with another mother who was not present often but came around enough. This woman's name is Patricia, but we called her Patri for short. She sat at the corner of the table next to Zipporah, directly across from me. Patri is beautiful, strong, smart, caring, intense and somewhat arrogant. Whenever she attended the dance class, she would display much confidence in her fitness, but also having fun. Patri is the definition of an Alpha female, like myself. Patricia is a great and dynamic woman who prides herself in her motherhood, health, body and her profession as a policewoman. She is a divorced mother with a daughter and a son both around Aaron and Abi's ages. I was not sure why she and Johnnie did not see eye to eye, but it was a comical interaction every time and I enjoyed observing them in action. These women all played a role in my integration into Utrera. They were always willing to help. Two seats down from me sat Mari Carmen Fernando, a beautiful, introverted, adorable, kind, loving and a little anxious woman. Mother of Amari's classmate and friend Eduardo, she also has a cute little daughter named Carmen. Her husband's name is Eduardo, who later became Amos's friend. I absolutely adore Mari Carmen and am intrigued by her timid spirit. She is the type of mother I was in the States. She keeps her life private from those not in her circle, but she also socializes and shows up for what's important to her. I admire that about Mari Carmen and how she is so easy to talk to. Sitting next to her was her sister, Inma Fernando. She is beautiful, kind, quiet, observant, and considerate. She is married to a sweet man named Manuel and they have a beautiful daughter, Mariola. The entire table was full of all strong, beautiful and loving women. Our comedian of the group, Teresa Santo, had me laughing all night.

"Tere!" she corrected me as I greeted her that evening. I laughed to myself thinking that she sounded similar to Lucy from *I Love Lucy*. This was an old comedy show I grew up watching. Tere and I both chuckled and gave our kisses. Tere is lovely, funny, moody, quirky and strong. Her husband is nice and nonchalant, and they have two daughters. Like many Andalusian Spanish women, Teresa loves to shop and takes pride in her appearance and clothes. To her left is Veronica Lopez, sitting quietly with a smile and a glass of wine. This woman has become very close to my heart. Vero is gorgeous, sweet, intelligent and spiritual. Zipporah and I instantly developed a very sacred bond with Veronica. She is a single mother of one beautiful daughter who is very special and bright. Vero has beautiful soft curly brown hair that looks like a little Afro! Her skin is pale yet slightly tan, due to her many cute brown freckles. She has insecurities and does not yet realize that she is absolutely gorgeous.

After we sat and ate at this large table in the Casa Diego restaurant, we decided it was time to migrate to another spot. We all split the bill, €20 per person. We were all full and had been drinking wine. We were at the restaurant for about three hours! Eating, talking, laughing and drinking. Afterward, we decided to go hang out at the Mini Bar. Exiting Casa Diego, we all walked about ten minutes toward the plaza. As we walked, we continued to laugh and talk. We hung outside the bar and ordered a few more drinks. Then we moved outside of the bar to a small table. Zipporah began talking to a big group of handsome young men that were sitting at the table next to ours. She boldly stepped into the center of the group and began a conversation with them as I talked to my friends. A few moments later, Zipporah approached Patri and me with a marijuana bud in her hand.

"Girl, smell this!" she insisted as she shoved it in my face.

"Mmmm. It smells good," I responded.

"Where did you get this!" Patri slowly demanded in English.

The combination of her intoxication, natural aggression and sense of police duties seemed strange. Confused, we stared at her with blank faces. She then began to reach into her purse in a hurry and for some odd reason I knew exactly what she was reaching for. Her police badge.

Annoyed but calm, I grabbed Patri's arm and pleaded, "Patri, no!"

But tipsy and aggressive, she snatched her arm out of my grip. She quickly stepped in front of the men and flashed her badge. The man who gave Zipporah the bud was young, incredibly handsome, tall, muscular and well dressed. He also spoke a little English. Suddenly the young man took out his official security badge and showed it to Patri. I found this a little amusing as it seemed like a "stand-off." But Zipporah did not think it was funny. She was embarrassed and upset with Patri. But Patri was still exchanging words with the young man. He did not care about her police badge. He just seemed like he wanted to pursue her. Zipporah expressed how mad she was and walked away. Mari Carmen followed Zipporah to make sure that she was OK. Shortly after, Patri and Zipporah talked. Marijuana is legal in the country of Spain but with certain discretions. It is illegal to consume it in public places. I understood and respected Patri's position. She is our friend, but she is also a policewoman and had an obligation to ensure we knew the law and were abiding by it. Yet, Zipporah and I could not comprehend how the law allows people to legally smoke chemically-based poisonous cigarettes, while frowning upon a natural plant that is grown from the earth. We quickly got over that little drama and continued our "tipsy late-night shenanigans."

Zipporah and I were then approached by what appeared to be a homeless man. Our friends had explained to us prior to his approach that this particular man used to be a famous clothing designer and known all throughout the entire country of Spain for his work. Sadly, over time he became addicted to drugs. He asked my sister and me for money, but my sister challenged him. She stated to him that he had to design her a dress if he wanted money. The young handsome man from earlier translated for her. The homeless man walked away and came back with a paper and pen in hand. Surprised yet excited, we watched him slowly draw on the paper as the other young man translated in Spanish what Zipporah was describing.

She then asked him, "How long will you allow for this drug to slowly kill you?" She called him out in love and not pity. I respected the homeless man for drawing the dress, but I was prouder of my sister for sending him that small piece of encouragement and tough love. The night was fun and eventful, and I was sore from laughing once I arrived home. I was happy to have had such a beautiful night with my sister and my new friends.

Nights like these began to happen often and some of the mothers and I became closer. The holidays passed and by this time, I was a permanent member of a group of mothers and friends who openly welcomed us into their regular daily routine of morning coffee after dropping the children off at school. The past two weeks I noticed a beautiful missing presence. It was Stella. For the past couple of weeks after the holidays Stella had not shown up for dance class or morning breakfast coffee. This one particular morning, I ran into her. We embraced with happiness to see one another. I genuinely asked how she was feeling. This question gave Stella an opportunity to open up to me. Stella shared with me that she had been diagnosed with a spinal condition. It was heartbreaking news because Stella was already battling scoliosis. Scoliosis is a spinal condition in which an individual is born with a curvature in their spine. It can be very painful. Therefore, finding out about her additional condition sent Stella into a small depression. Stella's father, her husband, Hugo and I were the only ones who knew of her condition. Stella let me know that she wanted to keep it that way for the time being. She told me that she hadn't been coming around lately because she needed time to process her news and feelings. She did not want to be pitied or treated differently by her friends. I complied and was honored that she trusted me enough to share that intimate detail with me. I then embraced her again and tried my best to encourage her with positive affirmations. I told her I believe that God gets the final say about one's life and medical conditions. Stella agreed. She guaranteed me that she is a strong warrior and will continue to fight and be happy. I feel like Stella often relied on her "motherhood" to draw her strength from. I'm convinced that every time she looked into Pelayo's beautiful brown eyes, it was a nonverbal power and survival exchange filled with love. This love between them brought Stella through some of the darkest moments in her life. Before we left each other, I promised Stella American "soul food." I assured her that the food would make both her soul and stomach feel much better! I told her that Amos and I would prepare her fried chicken. One of our mutual friends, Pedro, had bragged about Amos's fried chicken to Stella one day and she had requested it numerous times. Well, a friendly chicken dinner for Stella and her family turned into a full-on party at our house. Stella taught me that it is OK to lighten up on your pride and be vulnerable when you know that you are confiding in a trustworthy person. Sometimes releasing burdens off your chest can make any person feel much better, diminishing the feeling of loneliness. God is so good. He has a way of putting people into our lives at the perfect time. Stella was that for me as I know I was that for her. I enjoyed our conversations and our enlightening connection.

For example, on this particular Monday morning after finishing my regular routine, I ended up alone with Stella. I dropped my boys off at school and went to the usual café for coffee with my friends. The ladies and I conversed about different things. Eventually, each mother departed one by one, all having different errands to run. Finally, it was just Stella and me. Our conversation began with her sharing her past hurts and pains. This caused her to think and I could see her suddenly studying me in her head.

"What are you thinking about?" I asked, curious to know.

"Well," she began with her willingness to speak English.

I could gauge that she had a lot to say to me in particular.

"I think that you are a very positive and happy person. But I think that you and your sister have been through a hard and sad past. But that part of you is kept very ..."—Stella paused in search for the English word in her mind—"private," she finished with enthusiasm that she found the word.

"There are certain parts of you that you keep closed and private," Stella continued. Intrigued and surprised at her astounding truthful observation of me, I agreed. "You're right," I simply replied in Spanish.

Stella is normally very quirky and funny. But this particular conversation resonated with me because I was able to see the serious side of her. Stella was right about me. I had been so happy and at peace here in Spain that I refused to open up about my hurtful past. I felt as though that was perhaps Stella's way of telling me that she can see me even when I am not trying to be seen. I believe that she wanted me to be more comfortable to open up to her as she did to me. This short moment gave me more peace and comfort. Before leaving each other that morning, Stella and I had finally set a date for us to prepare dinner for her and her family. I told her, "Fried Chicken dinner at my house, next week, Saturday night. We will eat, drink, laugh and dance!" I also informed her that Tere and Conso A., along with their families, would be there as well. This made Stella even more excited.

The Saturday arrived for us to prepare that dinner and we did it together. Amos prepared the fried chicken and baked beans, Zipporah prepared the macaroni and cheese, and I prepared the kale salad. Everything came out perfect! We cleaned the house and set everything up. This night was full of fun and laughter. We had music playing, as the children played and jumped around in the living room. The adults all spent most of our time drinking and laughing in the dining area. We all tried sitting outside but the night was cold. It's sort of comical that all four of our husbands seemed sort of similar in personalities. Amos, Hugo, Antonio and Victor. They were all timid yet funny, quiet and extremely kind. However, once everyone became comfortable and secure, humor began to arise. This was the third house party that we'd had since we were in Spain. The sense of family and community is always present among our Spanish friends. When we all get together, we literally become one big family. If a child is hurt or cries it's not only the parents who come running to help but all parents come running. We all work collectively to make sure our families are all taken care of as a whole. Victor, the husband of Tere, was very observant but I could tell he enjoyed our company. He is gentle, nonchalant, quiet yet passionate. He adores his wife, Tere, and his two daughters. He's a hard worker and owns a print and copy shop here in Utrera. During our dinner house party, Conso A. and I ended up talking a little about her relationship with Antonio. Antonio was there and able to confirm or deny any allegations. This was when I first suggested to them both to read a book about love languages. In my encouragement for them to do, so I purchased two copies of the book *The Five Love Languages* by Gary Chapman. Antonio is a good man and I perceived him to be very observant. I can tell that he loves his wife and family and works hard to provide for them. I believe that his love language is "provision." Antonio may lack in affection but shows his love through providing for his family. Conso A.'s love language seems to be "affection," which can pose a slight strain on their relationship. She needs affection while he needs to provide. I informed them that they both needed to learn each other's language in order to survive as a couple. But they first needed the desire for the relationship to survive. It was nice counseling my friends and giving them advice in love and understanding. My relationship is not perfect, but we have had to make tough decisions for the betterment of our relationship. Through God's help, Amos and I have come a beautiful and long way as a couple, and we were both proud of our progression. The evening dinner turned out to be a blast and my family and I were happy to share a part of our culture with our friends. As the night wound down and everyone left, Amos and I decided that we needed to do this again with our other friends.

Within the next week the order for *The Five Love Languages* books arrived, and I was delighted and ready to meet the ladies for our morning coffee. I was anxious to give Conso A. her books. This particular morning, the ladies and I had coffee at a different bar because our usual bar La Bambina, had come under new management and was being renovated. We met at the Palodhu Gastrobar, owned by a beautiful couple, Consolación and Matias. Their bar later became one of my favorite places in Utrera. Matias is a true artist/chef and Consolación's service is always great.

Conso A. wanted to know how I was able to see the truth about her and her husband. She was perplexed about my discernment because she did not fully understand the meaning of the word, even though I feel as though she herself possesses the gift. We actually used the translator quite a bit for this conversation. She explained how she was surprised that I knew and could see that Antonio loved her dearly. However, he did not show it. She even mentioned that her younger son, Adrián, is very much like his father and also lacks the love language of affection. I then tried my best to explain how I discern an individual's spirit and not their looks. When I mentioned about the love languages again, I informed her that I ordered her and her husband two copies. Both in Spanish of course.

"They just arrived," I said with excitement in my voice. As she sat next to me, smiling at the two books, I could see she was also feeling emotional. Our other friends sitting at the table were curious about the book as well. She was excited and grateful. She then hugged and kissed me as everyone watched and adored this loving gesture. A few days later, Conso A. brought me a mason jar full of fresh honey. I believe it was her and Antonio's way of letting me know that they were appreciative of the books. I viewed it as a gift exchange.

The day finally arrived for us to have the next "American" dinner for our other group of Spanish friends. It was the beginning of March and a beautiful Friday evening. The weather was perfect as I cleaned and prepared to host the dinner indoors as well as outdoors. I loved how the Spanish enjoyed dining and spending time outdoors. This was also my favorite place to spend alone time, outside on my patio. Now I had the opportunity to share my space with our friends. Amos prepared his famous fried chicken wings along with hotdogs, homemade chips and his infamous sausage and cheese dip. At first, when everyone arrived it was relaxed. However, when everyone began to taste the food, the environment instantly changed! This was most of our guests' first time trying American food. They absolutely loved it! Emilia even continuously used the common Spanish phrase translated as "very delicious," to describe Amos's food. Although I did not help Amos cook, I felt equally happy and proud that they enjoyed our food so much. We all continued eating, laughing, talking, dancing and drinking. Maria from the Dominican Republic and her husband came as well. This was great because it was during the time Danny was going through health issues and he needed to get out and meet new people. I had a short conversation with Danny about how both he and José reminded me of each other. He asked me why. I explained as best as I could that they had a lot of similarities. Before even introducing them to one another, Jose and Danny both began talking and connecting that night.

Later, Danny came to me privately and joked, "You were right. You are a psychic!" Which was his way of saying that I have good intuition and discernment. He informed me that he was happy that he decided to join Maria. He admitted to needing this night as he was enjoying himself.

Maria and Fernando both enjoyed themselves as well. We conversed about differences in culture. One aspect of this conversation that shocked Maria and Fernando, was how common it was for Americans to get married at such a young age. This was strange to them. They objected that in Spain, adults typically settle down and have children at later ages ranging from thirty-five to forty years of age. We also discussed eating hours. As Americans we eat dinner between four to seven o'clock. But here in Spain dinner is not until ten o'clock through until midnight. My two sisters Zipporah and Maria lightened up the party with their lively and fun spirits. They began laughing and dancing together as others joined in. We all talked about our lives and languages as we shared music with one another. Because music is a universal language, it is always common to share music among friends and during gatherings. Natalia and José are usually limited on times spent outside of work or with their daughter. However, when they do step out, they cut loose and have a good time. I was glad to see them comfortable enough with my family and me to show us their party side. José even danced a little! It was a very funny sight to see and we all laughed. The children equally had fun. D'iona painted the girls' nails: Valeria, Victoria and Cayetana. Iván Luis and Amari played PS4 with Danny. The children all played and watched movies until they fell to sleep, each child scattered in their resting place throughout the living room. Glancing at my phone as I watched the children sleep, I noticed it was very late; it was around four in the morning. At the end of the night, we all sat in the dining room around the table and talked for a few more minutes before separating. Everyone said their goodbyes and went home tired, full and happy. Maria and Danny left first, next Natalia and José, then Emilia and Augustin. Last was Fernando and Maria. Another great observation of the night was that Danny was reluctant to come. He was still battling a bad stomach condition and did not want to be around a lot of people. However, Danny was finally diagnosed correctly and was slowly but surely starting to feel much better. This night at my house was his first time being out socially in months! My heart smiled as I watched him play video games with my son, laugh and converse with everyone. The next day Maria voiced how happy she was that Danny had such a great time. I was also happy to know them both and call them my friends.

The next Saturday afternoon was a scheduled BBQ with friends. This event was planned months in advance, so we were all excited to see each other. Zipporah was not feeling up to attending and stayed home. We arrived at the park around one thirty in the afternoon. This particular park was one of the largest parks in Utrera called the Quinto Centenario. The park had a little café and bar where parties and events were held. The day was beautiful and sunny. We were all dressed nicely in our casual attire. As we walked toward our friends, we began to get many stares. We then noticed our friends as we made our way through the park. It was one of those sunny but cool days. We were not the only family eager to take advantage of the beautiful weather. Many families were at this park on this particular Sunday! Jessica met me there and we all talked for a little while as I introduced her to the rest of my friends. She was happy to hang out and meet new people. Conso A. and Jessica got along great as well. Although Jessica did not stay long due to her family schedule, she made the best of the time she did spend with us. I was grateful she came. We finally greeted all of our friends that were there. It was good to see everyone, as we had not seen them in a while. It was a beautiful day and some interesting things happened. For example, as we approached and greeted all of my friends, I noticed Aaron was missing. I looked around and noticed his neon yellow T-shirt across the field close by with a large group of his classmates. They crowded around Aaron as they always did at school and hugged and kissed him. He smiled excitedly as he accepted their love. It was Cristina and her friends. I politely excused myself from my one group of friends as I went to say hello. They all welcomed me and offered me a beer that I could not refuse. We all talked for a few minutes. In the conversation, Anita exclaimed how my Spanish comprehension was very good. "Your understanding of Spanish is super good! You understand a lot!" she exclaimed with surprise and excitement. I tried to stay as humble on the outside as this did make me smile with pride on the inside. I chatted with them for a little while longer and then made my way back to my group of friends because I did not want to be rude. However, it was a pleasant surprise running into them.

    Dominican Maria came with her daughter, Claudia. She and everyone else were disappointed that Zipporah did not make it because she was the life of the party. Still, Maria socialized and had a great time with everyone. Most of our friends adore Maria, for she is always vibrant, friendly, outspoken and charming. Amos, Eduardo and Antonio were all working together to grill the meat and vegetables. Maria and I suddenly decided to get coffee at the bar nearby. She asked some of our friends what they wanted and Tere, Conso A. and Stella all ordered some coffee. They tried to pay Maria, but she refused. After we came back, I noticed that Mari Carmen was upset about something. She was offended because Maria had not personally asked her if she wanted coffee. She felt that to be rude since she asked the other ladies. I was extremely surprised yet amused by Mari Carmen's anger. She was adorable in her anger. Although I know she did not think it was funny, Mari Carmen felt disrespected. She considered Maria's actions, or lack thereof, to offer her a coffee were "very ugly." I tried to explain to Mari Carmen that it was not personal but a simple oversight. Nevertheless, we all had a great time. We all ate, the children played, and we danced and laughed until the sun set.

It was the beginning of February and the cold was dying down. Our dance class was receiving more recognition and I was happy to meet new women. On this day at dance class Conso A. put some wisdom in my ear. Our dance class was full this particular day, consisting of about four new people along with our ten faithful members. There was one particular beautiful woman whom Conso A. introduced me to. She specified that the woman was the mother of a child from Amari's class. However, when she said the name of the boy my heart skipped a beat. Paco Gomez was the same classmate that Amari encountered problems with for months. Nevertheless, I politely kissed her in the tradition and introduced myself. She was very nice with a kind face and spirit. But for the entire class that day, my mind stayed focused on Paco and his mother. After the class session ended, I saw her and my sister laughing and making each other's acquaintance. The class members socialized with each other after the session and I was approached by Conso A. and Stella. They talked with me about dancing and working out but to be honest my mind was stuck on Paco Gomez and his mother. As I watched my sister happily converse with her from the side of my eye I had to know! Was this the mother of Paco Gomez? I then pulled out my translator and discreetly asked Conso A. She reluctantly answered that she was. At that moment I tried to hide my anger but could not. Conso A. saw the flash of anger in my eyes and calmly told me to "wait and stay calm." I asked her if she thought it a good idea if I said something to Paco's mother about his harassment of my son, but Conso A. repeated that I should wait. As I spent the next few moments calming my emotions, I attempted to understand Conso A.'s intentions. Then Conso A. gave me a great perspective while walking to the school to retrieve our children. Essentially, Conso A.'s spirit was teaching me a beautiful lesson and Zipporah confirmed it. Everything happens for a reason. God puts people in our lives for a purpose and it was not by chance that Paco Gomez's mother came to our dance class and we all ended up liking each other. I also learned that just because our children fight, it does not mean that the parents are not allowed to be friends. We are the adults and by us displaying friendliness to one another, we are showing our children a different way. Conso A. did not say this exactly; however, that is the message that my spirit received from her. Conso A. often surprised me and I was thankful to receive her wisdom. Our conversation eased my mind and heart as I felt a powerful shift within me.

It was always a pleasure spending time with my Spanish friends. However, I would often miss connecting with my fellow Americans. Here in Utrera there are many Americans living in town due to the airbase. Because Amos worked on the base, we were able to make connections with some of the military members and company employees. Jessica is a military spouse, yet I met here because her son attended Salesianos. This caused us to link and see each other often. On the other hand, meeting my other American friends, Jennifer, Annette, Toni and Terrance was in a different scene. Each connection was unique and special.

I can recall when I first heard about Jennifer from Amos. Jennifer was Amos's colleague. She, Annette and Terrance all work for the same company. A few months prior, she shared with Amos that she desired some fellow "melanated sisters to hang out with."

"I got a wife and a sis at the house," Amos responded in a funny tone.

Within the next weekend we invited Jennifer to a house party. Jennifer is a very strong-willed and outspoken middle-aged woman. She loves to travel and socialize. She is extremely talkative, yet fun, sweet, stern, brash, a little obnoxious, bossy and extremely funny. I liked her because she speaks her mind like I do. After a delicious dinner prepared by my favorite chef, Amos, we sat outside and had drinks. Jennifer and Zipporah became more comfortable with one another as they cracked jokes and laughed. I was delighted to have met Jennifer and we made it our purpose to stay connected. One day Jennifer was having a barbecue at her house with coworkers and friends and she invited my husband and me. It was the same day and time that Amari and D'iona attended Greta's birthday party. We dropped them off and left the little ones at Tia Patri's house and headed to Jennifer's barbecue. Her profession is a chef and her home was beautiful and well prepared to entertain. It was mostly Americans there. One of the Americans was married to a Spanish woman and she caught my attention with her bright personality. Her name was Rosa. Rosa had a sister visiting from Madrid and her name was Maria. My conversation with Rosa's sister Maria was most enjoyable because her spirit was patient and kind, assisting me in practicing my Spanish. The barbecue was fun and we all had a great time. As most of the guests began to depart, a few of us stayed behind to talk, laugh and dance a little more. In time Jennifer became like family to us and the connection was something we both needed.

The next time I saw Jennifer was at the first company dinner held in Seville. We were happy to see one another as well as see other Americans attending. I not only socialized with Jennifer and others, but there was another queen there around Jennifer's age who I became drawn to. Her name is Annette. She is a middle-aged Black American woman who works on the airbase. She is tall, beautiful and has the most gorgeous and healthy dark brown skin that I've ever seen. Her exterior is serious, but her heart is kind and pure. She is wise and does not tolerate nonsense. I initially met this powerful woman in August 2018 during the feria. But this night, at the dinner I was able to get to know her a little better. We instantly clicked and she made it known that she liked me. Annette is a very private person, so I felt honored she even liked me. She is older and God has a funny way of always putting older women into my life to be a small voice of wisdom. We exchanged numbers and made a promise to meet again. The next meeting was a hair appointment Annette made with Zipporah. She wanted braids but needed a full hair treatment first. Zipporah did not hesitate to take her as a customer and I assured my sister she would love Annette. That day became like a family reunion because not only did Zipporah invite me to come over and spend time with them during Annette's appointment, but one of Zipporah's closest friends from Florida was also in town. It was more of a lady's day to just sit, talk and laugh. Chelle is a beautiful, strong and talented Haitian American woman. She and Zipporah were very close, and I was glad they were friends. When I first met her, it was not pleasant because Zipporah selfishly invited her two weeks before moving into her own place. I do not mind having company at my house as long as I know the person and I am aware. I was not aware of Chelle's need to stay at my house at the time and I was livid. Zipporah and I even had a bad argument about it but quickly resolved it.

During her two weeks in my house, Chelle and I got to know one another. I observed that she knew Zipporah very well and could agree with me on certain aspects I felt Zipporah could change. In the end we all bonded. This small situation taught Zipporah, Chelle and me many valuable lessons. I was grateful to know Chelle and I was sad to see her leave after three long months of bonding. I was going to miss her beautiful singing and her willingness to connect with my children.

I can recall the night we all went out before she left. That same day Chelle was contacted by her family to give her unfortunate news about her two aunts. Her most favorite aunt passed away and the other was in intensive care and fighting for her life. Chelle took the news really hard because both aunts were like mothers to her. Zipporah and my family comforted her during this hard time and purchased her flight home. We all decided to have a two-night dancing spree of fun and positivity to lift Chelle's spirit. I called Tia Patri to babysit for both nights. Tia Patri developed a beautiful and permanent bond with our children and we are like family. I was always appreciative of her willingness to care for our children.

Friday night we arrived at the X-Central around eleven thirty. We were literally the only four customers there. The bartender was a nice young man from Brazil. We liked that no one was there because it felt as though we were VIPs. After settling at our spot and ordering drinks, we began to request our music and dance. We all had a wonderful time dancing and drinking the entire night. We met a few others that came into the bar and they all had the same concept. Drink and dance. The night finally came to an end. We walked Chelle and Zipporah home and headed to our house.

The next night Dominican Maria came out with us. We had such a good time! We drank and danced all night. We started out at X-Central again since we had such a great time the night before. As soon as we got upstairs, we ran into others from the previous night. One of the mothers of the group was so excited to see us. She attempted to introduce us to everyone with her, from her husband to all of her group of friends. Some greeted us with love and others simply stared like deer. Her young daughter dragged us on stage to dance to people singing karaoke. That night we all danced until we sweated, met new people and exchanged numbers. Afterward, we decided to head to another club named Morgan's. When we arrived, the scene was full of excitement. We found the perfect table near the front side of the club. Amos ordered drinks while we all danced. We could see many people watching us from near and far, yet we kept dancing and enjoying our last moments with Chelle.

We also shared time with our other American friends Toni and Terrance at a dinner they hosted. The first time I met this beautiful couple was through Zipporah. Toni was an active member of Coliseum Gym where Zipporah and I hosted our dance class. I remember seeing Zipporah talking in English to this young woman with long beautiful dark hair. They were speaking as if they knew one another in the past. I walked over and introduced myself. She informed us that her husband is an American firefighter on the airbase. We talked, showed pictures and exchanged numbers. Toni even joined our class that evening and enjoyed it. We all made plans to link in the future so we could meet her husband, Terrance.

Later, Toni invited us to her house for a dinner and we were all happy to accept the invitation. When we arrived, I instantly noticed how lovely their house was. The decor was elegant, and they possessed many portraits up for others to enjoy. They also had a cute puppy named Boa. Toni and Terrance were conservative people and did not socialize often. Therefore, there were not many people invited to this dinner and I appreciated the intimate time we all spent. Toni only invited Amos, me, Zipporah and Jennifer who came later that night. Toni cooked some of her Filipino dishes and it was delicious. We all enjoyed each other's company and became great friends from that point on. When I first met Terrance, I was not sure how to receive his serious look. Time progressed and I realized that he is simply a very funny teddy bear. Terrance is a tall, handsome, hilarious, "good old country boy." He makes my family and me laugh every time we are around him. Their love story was another I had to note in my journal. Integrity was what helped Toni fall in love with Terrance. Toni was in line at the grocery store with a few people in front of her. She noticed the man being checked out in front of her. The cash register was showing one of his products as one price while the true price was on the actual tag. Terrance pointed out that he was actually being charged less. Toni remembered checking Terrance out in this moment and thinking that he was a handsome and honorable man. She was already in love. Eventually they got married and moved to Spain for Terrance's job. I truly enjoyed hearing how Toni and Terrance met and I was thankful for this evening. We had a wonderful time and planned to do it again.

Time seemed to move faster as each month passed with no remorse. There was always an event to attend or something to do for the children. My times spent with my family and friends were very important. Tina's family and ours became like a tribe. We began to travel together, eat out often and every week they were at my house. I was happy to have them all and God knew that I needed them. To show our appreciation, my family and I decided to have a nice little birthday dinner for Tina because she meant so much to us. It was on a Saturday night that Tina and her family came over for dinner. We only invited a few of Tina's friends because we wanted it to be more personal and private. There was Tina's family, of course, and her boyfriend, Alfonso, whom we all adored. It was simple but nice. Amos grilled meat while Zipporah and I prepared vegetables and macaroni and cheese. After we all ate dinner, we presented Tina with her gift. It was a beautiful collage of photos of our families together. Tina and everyone else loved it. As we sat outside, I shared with Tina how I was discouraged about the progress of my Spanish speaking. I also expressed to her that I was feeling like my mind hit a "plateau." She gave me her heartfelt encouragement. She shared how both she and her mother, Tia Patri, were impressed by my comprehension of Spanish and my rapid learning ability. She also emphasized that her mother would often come home bragging about my Spanish.

"And you have been here only one year, Joy! Wow! That is amazing," Tina professed to me in English.

She made me feel so much better. This night was all about Tina, yet she found a way to give me a gift of inspiration. We danced to Tina's favorite music and played with the children. The food and cake were amazing, and I could tell everyone had a beautiful time. It was times like these that reminded me of why my family and I are here. We are here to connect, learn and grow.

I relished moments of edification with my friends because I enjoyed learning. However, I also have a need to feel secure in that learning, and sometimes I do not. I can remember discussing my discomfort in my Spanish learning process with my friends Natalia and José. It was Friday evening and I had just dropped Amari at his evening after-school program. As I strolled down the sidewalk, I passed several of the cafés located across from the school. I spotted Natalia and her husband José. I had not seen them in a while, and it showed in the excitement of our greeting. We hugged and kissed as they offered me to join them for coffee. I didn't want to impose especially if they wanted time alone, yet they both insisted. We sat there and pleasantly conversed about many different aspects of life. This time with Natalia and Jose gave me a chance to learn about them both more intimately. José was born in Andalusia but raised predominantly in Madrid. Meanwhile, Natalia is from northern Spain. This difference in environment gave them both unique perspectives on the Spanish culture. This was interesting to hear, for they agreed on most subjects yet disagreed on others.

I considered José to be one of my good English-speaking friends. He would always give me advice and tips on how to improve my Spanish. I was always appreciative of his encouragement. We all talked about various subjects. Life, our children, school schedules, my search to purchase a home in Utrera, and so on. I specifically remember us discussing the weather. Both José and Natalia were glad to give me a little Spanish lesson as we sat and socialized, sipping coffee. I had my small notebook with me that I used to write and memorize Spanish phrases. As the lesson began, I started to write down the different words and types of weather phrases that they taught me. When they completed the small lesson, the conversation shifted to the subject of their relationship. I probed and asked them how they met. José was in his early twenties and in the military, while Natalia was slightly older and in a professional administrative position. They both proclaimed that one day they locked eyes. That same day they went on a date. After the first date they were both inseparable. They dated long distance in the early years of their relationship. Eventually they got married and built a beautiful life together with their daughter, Greta. I enjoyed listening to their love story. This led us to the conversation of sex. There was a lot of smiling and laughter among us about this particular subject. They taught me phrases that I could use. One particular phrase that I loved was *me pones*, which translates to "you put me." This phrase had two different meanings. The first meaning was explained with many red cheeks and giggles as they both spoke in English. "You turn me on." The second was "Oh my gosh, it is such a pleasure getting to know you! I love you already!" The second phrase was used when you meet a person you have an instant connection with. This I noted because I was experiencing many instant connections while here in Spain. We all laughed at the humor of each phrase. I thanked them both for this beautiful encounter as a major lesson stuck in my head.

    José taught me to always go out and use the new words and phrases that I learned in Spanish. It wasn't until almost eight months later when I felt comfortable enough to use that particular phrase with a connection that I made. Her name is Mariali. I met her at a professional functional recovery center in town. Mariali is a physical therapist and performed my service. I was excited to meet another "sister." As she performed my service we talked like old friends. She shared with me that her father is Afro-Latino from South America, while her mother is from

Utrera. There was an instant and beautiful connection between Mariali and me. Although Mariali did not know much about her African lineage, I knew that our "blackness" is what bonded us. Mariali is absolutely beautiful both physically and in spirit. Her skin is golden caramel, and her hair is dark brown and extremely curly. She possessed a certain strength and I later found out why, once we became friends. She is married with two beautiful children, Miriam and Adrian. Her husband is the owner of three different great local restaurants in Utrera. Mariali is beautiful, honest, strong, intelligent and a great mother. Her children became great friends with all three of my children. Once we both became more acquainted, we made time for the children to meet and play often.

My first observation of Mariali was that she had many acquaintances but few of whom she considered close. She was so comfortable in who she is, and her only focus seemed to be her family. This led me to ask her questions. I asked her how it was growing up in this small town as a young girl with caramel skin and dark curly hair. As I mentioned before, Utrera is a small town and there are not many people of melanin. Thinking about my question, Mariali squinched her face in memory as she explained that she was discriminated against by her peers all her life. This in turn, made her build an emotional wall to protect herself. Nevertheless, like my own childhood history, Maria's negative experience with discrimination made her a stronger and wiser woman. Each time we went out together in public, I would always admire her confidence and strength. Mariali and I became very comfortable with each other as well as our children. She spoke and understood a little English while I spoke and understood more Spanish. Nonetheless, we frequently practiced with one other. Israel, the husband of Mariali, is tall, handsome, friendly and an absolutely great chef. His passion for cooking is admirable. I love discussing food with him, as well as Amos. I was grateful for this connection with Mariali and her family.

I continued learning and connecting with the people of Spain as well as learn about the entire country itself. There were many cities Amos and I wanted to visit as we made concrete plans to do so. I not only traveled with my husband and family, but I made time to have "sister trips" with Zipporah for she is also my friend. One of my best. This year for her birthday we planned a trip to Rota, a small town in the southern province of Cadiz. This town was considered a military beach town. During this time many of the ferias were beginning. Zipporah and I decided to take the train and meet Dominican Maria there. We planned to stay for one night and return the next morning.

My mind wondered as I anxiously sat on the train. Maria had already been waiting for us in Rota because she was bartending throughout the feria weekend. I received a troubling message from Maria while we were on our way to the train station. She explained that she got into a bad disagreement with one of her coworkers and as a result she was fired. Maria was upset, for she felt she was wrongfully mistreated. She called to inform Zipporah and me that she was leaving. Already in route, I frantically called her back to see if she was OK. She sounded sad and a little distraught. I reassured her that we were still on our way and not to worry. I asked her to go to our hotel to calm down and wait for us there, and she complied. By the time we arrived,

Maria met us both in the waiting lodge and led us to the room to get dressed. Finally, after we reached the Rota Feria it was around ten thirty in the evening as the festivities had already begun. Maria felt much better as we were all happy to celebrate Zipporah's birthday in this way. Maria explained to us more about the coworker who she had the altercation with.

We were all dressed very nicely and ready to have a great time. When we got to the feria Maria's spirit was instantly lifted. It was satisfying seeing and feeling festive energy surrounding the event. The scenery was very beautiful, bright and cultured. The night was lit with many colorful decorative streetlights. Perhaps the most beautiful part of the feria was the vivid imagery of cross-culturalization. Rota is near a military installation; therefore, many Americans live in the area. Some were dressed as normal Americans while others were dressed in traditional flamenco attire. Everyone's fashion ranged from formal to casual. The environment was peaceful, lively and positive. It was pure fun as we hopped from one tent to the next, drinking and socializing with new people.

We met many people from different walks of life in each tent. We then ironically ended up at Maria's old tent where she was originally working. Her boss felt bad about the situation and called her to come. When we arrived he gave us VIP treatment. We met the DJ as her boss set our table up nicely on the side of the stage. We all toasted to Zipporah reaching a new year. We ended our night in that same tent. We danced and laughed the entire time. Maria was happy to be enjoying the feria while the coworker who insulted her was working and serving tables. It was a great and funny irony. Around two o'clock we were all ready to end the night and sleep. We walked to the hotel, talking loud and reminiscing. When we finally reached the hotel, we all crashed on the large bed. What a night, I thought to myself in Spanish the next morning. The more time I was in Spain the more I thought, dreamed and spoke the language. We all got dressed and headed out. We caught the train back to Utrera as we continued to laugh and joke about the amazing night we had together. There were many nights like these with my family as well as friends. I was ready to continue my journey exploring Spain, each time I met a new city. It was nice seeing other Americans at events for it sometimes felt like home. Making friends with others who share the same language can be a deeper and more secure relationship, while the relationships made with the Spanish can be at times more challenging because of the language barrier. However, I have always been a queen who likes to be challenged. I valued each person in my life and held on to the lessons learned from them all. I appreciated all of my connections here and assessed my purpose in each of their lives.

    I can remember meeting a young American woman through Zipporah. Zipporah was like me in this aspect, but more social. She enjoyed meeting new people and whenever we went out, she made a new acquaintance. This young woman's name is Tazjaa. She is a beautiful twenty-something year old American firefighter from the base. Zipporah met her at her job and they became friends. We met her on Saturday when Zipporah invited her to a water park in Seville with the children. Zipporah was always taking the kids whenever she could to be thoughtful. I immediately liked Tazjaa's energy when we first met. She is young but very confident and seemed to have a good head on her shoulders. She is biracial but seems to connect more to her black roots. Her mother is Black American, and her father is White American. Talking and getting to know Tazjaa was interesting. I enjoyed listening to her talk about her upbringing and her overall experiences in life.

I was a little shocked about her experience here in Spain. Tazjaa was one of the first female firefighters on base and she broke some sort of record. She confessed to us that her fellow firefighters both American and Spanish were not welcoming toward her, at first. In fact, they were unfriendly and would not even greet her. Part of it was sexism because she is a young woman who had already made a career for herself. However, part of it I suspected was that some of these men were older with over twenty years of firemen experience. They may be making ignorant assumptions about this young black female whom they knew nothing about. Perhaps they felt that the young American firemen and women possessed an unfair sense of entitlement and privilege simply because they are American. Perhaps in their eyes, the respect for her needed to be earned and not given. Of course, this was my theory but only time would tell. My theory proved to be true. Later that summer, Tazjaa mentioned to me that at a recent luncheon was the first time that she felt included. They actually included her in their conversation. This to me, sounded like gradual progress. Zipporah and Tazjaa became friends as well as our family. This particular Saturday afternoon, Zipporah and Tazjaa took our children to Isla Mágica, a water park located in Seville. This gave Amos and me time to spend alone and I was grateful. It was nice simply spending alone time with Amos because he worked a lot. The children had an absolute blast with Zipporah and Tazjaa and we were very appreciative of them both!

I always enjoy time with other people, but I mostly enjoy time alone. I was in need of a pedicure and manicure, so I asked the ladies for help. Teresa recommended me to her close friend Rocio. Zipporah and I met her in late June. She had such a beautiful and sweet energy about her. They all shared with me that she is a nail technician and showed me her beautiful work. That day we exchanged numbers and I contacted her the very next week. She was very sweet to squeeze me into her schedule. Rocio greeted me with excitement when I arrived. She introduced me to her sister who is a hairdresser at their shop. Rocio escorted me to the back room, which was small yet elegantly decorated. The walls were embellished with royal dark lavender. The store had a modern trimming of white Moroccan designs. Pictures of sample nail work were displayed on the wall. The energy was very relaxing. Rocio didn't speak or understand much English, which was fine for me. While I still struggled in actually speaking Spanish, my comprehension of Spanish was quite good. Rocio and I talked about life, our children, school, work, and so on. I learned that Rocio had a million cousins in Utrera. For example, my favorite neighbor, Ms. Conso, was the second cousin of Rocio. I knew this because Ms. Conso was eager to explain to me her relationship with Rocio after she saw social media posts of us all out together. This both surprised and tickled me. Overall, I enjoyed my conversation with Rocio. She did a beautiful job on my hands. I chose a pale teal color and she added golden dressing on my thumb and ring fingers. I loved it so much that I decided to make Rocio my new nail technician, while she also became my friend. It was a pleasant experience as are many I have encountered while living in Spain. My lovely interactions and relationships with people have not only brought light to my experience here, but it has also brought me peace, love and understanding.

Chapter 4:

My Loves and Hates of Spain

My life's journey here in this urban country has given me more perspective on life. As did many of my past experiences in other countries. Amos and I have found ourselves loving many things about Spain. However, there are features we detest and would change if we could. Being a stay-at-home mother for many years has its pros and cons. Living in Spain as a stay-at-home mother definitely does not fit the description of those mothers who profess to be bored and unmotivated. At least not for me. Towns like Utrera treasure the children and it shows during the school year, holidays, summer break, and so on. I can say that I honestly appreciate that aspect of smaller towns because life seems more fun and freer, like the heart of a child. I have worked hard to give my children a more fulfilling childhood than my own. Becoming an active mother in the school community has not only broadened my horizons, but it has built more character within me. From school projects to plays, I have truly enjoyed this change. Meanwhile, there are ideas I would love to discard. For example, school projects for the younger grades are often done by the parents. We all come together as if we were in school ourselves and complete the task as one team. Although these are fun, it can also be a challenge in some ways. Aaron, being my only child in a younger grade during the first school year, had been given many projects as such.

One day Aaron's class was given a project to familiarize the children with the human anatomy. His entire class was broken down into groups. Each group was given a part of the body to create and then display together. Aaron's particular group was tasked with the muscles. I was not yet fluent in Spanish; therefore, one of the parents, Cristina, ensured I was understanding my task completely. Although she was not a member of my group, she knew I would have questions and she was willing to answer them. Later I met Anita, mother of twins, Xavier and Martina B. She reached out to me about the project. The consensus was to meet at her house at nine thirty in the morning to complete a clay display of muscles on a big diagram poster. There were four mothers total in the group: me, Anita, Ana, and Aika. We ended up having a nice time laughing and getting to know each other. We all wanted to spend more time together; therefore, we decided to go out for coffee. Although the day was cold and raining, we did not mind grabbing our umbrellas and walking to a cafe nearby. There was a funny awkward moment when we sat quietly looking at each other in silence. Aika suddenly exclaimed with her arms up and waving,

"Americano!"

We all burst into laughter! Aika and I were both grateful to have a fellow English-speaking mother to converse with. I was equally delighted about the outcome of the project and how well we worked together. This helped me to understand teamwork on another level than the one with my family. I did not know these women yet; we all came together for a common goal and executed the task beyond my expectations. I loved Anita's vigorous personality and hefty laughter. Anita's carefree and cheerful personality simply inspired me every time I was around her. She always seemed to bring air into a stuffy room. Experiences like these assist me in my growing desire to make a home in Spain, while other experiences cause me to wonder.

Later that evening when I arrived to retrieve Aaron, his teacher inquired about my project meeting with the mothers. She wanted to know the outcome. I told her that I enjoyed myself and it was good getting to know some of the other mothers. I was appreciative because her inquiry showed me that she cared. Perhaps she was nervous about my integration with the other mothers, as was I. Aaron's first year in school has been substantially helpful toward his overall progression. I could discern that Aaron enjoyed his daily routine of school, as did Amari.

The time arrived to attend the quarterly meeting held for the parents to discuss progression and upcoming events with the teachers. Sitting and observing this meeting, I became annoyed and confused. There was so much rapid Spanish speaking in my ear and many accents to interpret, yet I could not. Translating as much as I could in my head, I noticed that some parents understood the times and dates permitted for the next event.

While other parents attested and were upset because they would be at work during that time. One teacher could not calm the oppositions of over twenty parents; therefore, the meeting was like a busy stockroom full of brokers all calling out numbers at once. I sat quietly as I jotted down the dates and times for this next event. Thinking to myself, I hoped that this meeting's outcome was not a normal situation. It lacked order and organization and that made me anxious. When I left the meeting, I was a little confused and was forced to ask another parent for help. Vanessa, the sweet and beautiful mother of Adrian and my neighbor was happy to help. That was one aspect of living in Spain that I disliked and always felt vulnerable. I did not enjoy asking for help because I have always valued my independence. Living in a country where 27.7 percent of people speak my language sometimes posed challenges and created various obstacles. Nevertheless, there is never a challenge I would back down from unless it was harmful to me or my family.

I believe we all reap what we sow, and I choose to sow seeds of happiness, respect and love. However, sometimes I may not receive that same treatment back. Many of my American friends living in Spain possess similar complaints as my husband and I do. For example, the idea that all Americans are rich. I believe that many Americans experience a form of economic inequality. This is an aspect of living in Spain that I hate the most. Many people in this country, along with other countries, assume that all Americans live comfortably and lack a necessity to worry about money. Especially the American military. It is a known fact that the American government provides housing funds for military members. Unfortunately, various realtor companies and local homeowners throughout various countries have taken advantage of this knowledge. Americans are charged double, sometimes triple in currency in comparison to how much a citizen of that particular country pays for housing. This is unjust and unfair to all Americans military or not. From a personal perspective many people in Utrera assume that my family and I are American military members because Amos works on the airbase. And as mentioned before while we all (Amos, Zipporah and I) proudly served our country in the past, we are now US civilians. Therefore, we do not receive house funding from the government. Thus, we all pay for our housing and other bills the same as any citizen of the city. From an income earned through hard work. Not only is this inequitable, but it also places a strain on our need and desire to save more. I hated the feeling of how our Spanish friends would cringe when they find out how much we pay for rent. Many of them have even warned us about how Americans are overcharged for certain things. Nevertheless, we are grateful and blessed to be able to live a comfortable lifestyle while we are not rich. We have bills and financial responsibilities just like everyone else. No matter the amount we pay, whether less or more; the fact is that we are making an honest contribution to the country's economy. I have even noticed on occasions, being charged extra at bars, markets, and so on. The people see us and assume we are unaware of their need to make extra from us. Yet I am here to say that I notice and choose to keep the peace. My family and I have endured many hardships and pain to build the life we possess presently. This fact caused me to scream inside as I think of the ignorance of those assuming all Americans have a perfect life. However, what others need to understand is that some US military families are low-income and/or poor. Some live paycheck to paycheck. I believe treatment of equality is important and shows character. Euros are almost double to our US dollar. Not only are we being charged a higher rent, but we are also paying more because of the currency difference. I ask myself if it is legal to overcharge a person based upon their nationality. Perhaps the Spanish government is unaware. Either way, it is unfair and one of my greatest dislikes about Spain. In the end, God said in His Word that "vengeance is mine." When one knowingly executes unjust actions, that unjustness will be reciprocated. This is a top reason for my desire to purchase a home instead of renting. Within the first year and a half of living in Spain my husband and I knew that this was a place where we could settle and raise our children. Giving them the opportunity to learn a new language while overcoming obstacles as English-speaking black children. I want my children to be strong and well-rounded, as does my husband. Yet the process for buying a home in Spain as a noncitizen also posed to be unfair and overly strict. Although I understand the reasoning, I hate that this way exists within the process. Nevertheless, as I always state, we put our best foot forward and tried finding and purchasing a home in Spain.

Before beginning my house hunt, I began gathering information needed to understand the process of purchasing property in Spain. I also consulted with my local friends. My girlfriend Maria Lopez was extremely helpful. She took me to the realtor office of her friend Susana, the realtor and owner. When Maria introduced us, she was proud to inform me of this information. Susana was very professional, and friendly. Accompanying her was a co-realtor assisting her. Maria translated to Susana exactly what I was looking for: a large five-bedroom, three-bath home that is close to the children's school while close to our current community pool. Susana wrote down every detail and promised to get back to me that afternoon or evening. Susana kept her promise. She asked Maria to inform me that she found three homes she wanted to show me later that same evening. I gladly accepted. Without hesitation I asked Zipporah to watch the children until Amos returned from work. Susana and her co-realtor met me at the first house. It was very close to our current home. I immediately fell in love with this house because of its number. It was a house number seven. Many people know that seven is a sacred number. Those who know me personally know that it is my favorite number. Whenever I am in contact with or notice this number, I am alert. For example, I was the seventh born child; I was born in July, the seventh month of the year; my king, Amos, and I were married in 2007. Consequently, this house immediately caught my attention. The owner was a middle-aged petite kind looking woman. She had a daughter who spoke English above average. Susana introduced us as the owner was happy to show me around. I felt love at first sight with just the very first home! In a perfect scenario I would purchase this home immediately. It met all of my requirements plus more. The entrance was separate with the stairs on the right. The stairwell was a nice grayish marble and less steep than usual stairs. They seemed much safer for my small children. There was a half bathroom to the left of the foyer with a large pantry and garage to the left of the entrance. This could solve our constant parking issues, I thought to myself. Past the entrance, there was a huge living area with a grand open space. There was a large beautiful wooden dining table setting toward the front. Then there was a large sofa to the other side of the space, and a wide sliding door that led to a nice and spacious two-section patio. It was perfect for my family and me. The top section of the patio possessed a seating area suitable for up to six persons or more. Meanwhile, the lower section was perfect for my children's playtime. I was already mentally preparing this home for my family and myself, strategically replacing their furniture, paintings and homewares with mine. As I was glancing at this patio, the owner's daughter began to share with me her great memories of many festivities on that very patio. This gave me more confidence as I could easily imagine my own gatherings on this patio. The kitchen was toward the left side of the house. It was connected to the open living space. The kitchen was very open with many cabinets. There was even a nicely designed breakfast nook where an additional dining set was placed. The windows were large enough to use as sliding doors. They led out to the back patio as well. I ventured back out to the patio from the window. Squinting my eyes, I looked up at the sun, adoring its breathtakingly radiant light.

    The owner then led me up the stairs where all of the bedrooms were located. There was a wide-open space that connected all of the four bedrooms. Each room was spacious with natural lighting and oversized windows for fresh breezes. The master bedroom had me sold! It was enormous with a beautiful fireplace and miniature library! It was sizeable enough to have an office desk as well as an entire king-size bedroom setting. It even had an attached patio that led to an outside addition to the house. This addition was a large storage room where the washer and dryer were situated. On the third floor from that storage room was a small in-law suite. This was a unique addition to the house that the owners completed on their own. I envisioned a music and/or recording studio for our family instead of the in-law suite. It was perfect for our family and I wanted it. I secretly felt as though we did not need to search any further. However, I also knew one of the best rules to house hunting. Always look at multiple homes before making a decision. I continued on the house tour with Susana and the co-realtor.

The second home was also lovely and met all my requirements and more. It was huge and I considered it to be a small mansion. There were three floors and the biggest courtyard I have ever seen in a home! Looking around the courtyard I spotted a mini chicken barb in the backyard. The house extended to a different side of the street. The only downfall about this home was that it required a 100% percent renovation. But this home was so large and beautiful that I saw its enormous potential. When I envisioned my family in this home, I could see multiple generations all in this beautiful estate. We could use it as a home, a restaurant, a club, a studio, an art expo, or all of the above. The sky was the limit with this property. I liked it even more as we continued the tour. I jotted down my notes for both homes, yet my heart remained set on the first house. Nevertheless, this realtor did her job and kept her word of finding me just want I needed and wanted. I was ready to see the last home so I could go home and discuss it all with Amos.

The third and final house was also very tasteful. However, it was much further away from my current home than I would have preferred. It was a beautiful modern home with a front and backyard space. There was a reasonably sized basement that caught my attention. I was very impressed with Susana. Within the first time of her meeting me, she was able to find two homes that exceeded all of my requirements. I was amazed! After viewing each house, I had much to discuss with Amos. I was equally excited to tell him and Zipporah about these homes. Susana drove me back to my home and I informed her that I would first talk with my husband then contact her.

My family and I were able to view the first house together and they equally adored it. Conclusively, after visiting multiple banks while learning the process of purchasing property in Spain, our house buying dreams came to a temporary pause. I realized that it was too soon to buy and Utrera may not be the place we call home. I learned to be more patient when making a decision so permanent. With that lesson, my husband and I decided to wait and look for a larger home to rent. We started our search. God divinely worked it out where an American family was moving out of the home in the next street over from our current home. And even though I felt in my heart that we still faced economic inequality with the new landlord, he showed kindness and the house was much better. It was more spacious, a better location, with additional upgrades and closer to the pool. We gave our current landlord thirty-days' notice and we moved into our new home by mid-summer. This home was an answer to our prayers. It was the same housing neighborhood, better parking, an extra office space, a large attic, and a more open living area and kitchen. The master bedroom had a beautiful upgraded separate bathroom, and all the windows were screened in (which is very uncommon here in Spain). We all felt so blessed and much happier in our new home! After settling into the new house, I began to meet my neighbors. They were all older than I was yet kind and welcoming. They were not hesitant to speak to me and inform me of the many festivities of the town.

The people here seem to be happy and content with their daily lives. During the holidays is when I felt I could see my children living in this town for a longer period of time. Nonetheless, the holidays are the happiest times of the year. I have observed that most small towns like Utrera take great pride in the festivities of the holiday season. The city turns into a light show. This would be considered one of my largest pros to living in Spain. Whether we visit a larger city or smaller town, the spirit of the holidays is always joyful and lively. My new neighbors as well as all of our friends had been telling us about this particular parade, which occurs during their traditional celebration called "Three Kings." Andalusia seemed to have many different parades, processions and celebrations throughout the year. This was the *cabalgata de los reyes magos*, the parade of the kings. It seemed to be everyone's favorite. The streets would be packed with people from adults to teens to babies, all ready to review and receive. Floats with different themes and characters would march through the small streets, tossing candy and surprisingly great gifts. I was informed by my friends that many families, companies and groups would begin financial, physical and mental preparation for this parade a year prior. Thousands of euros would be spent from the pockets of those not caring about the money, but happy to honor the tradition and the culture. I have observed that Spaniards take much pride in their customs; therefore, whatever they may do, it is always done with pride and dignity. During the day of the parade my family, friends and I walked to the plaza around six o'clock. My children were all excited, but mostly Amari and D'iona. We were catching the late evening parade; therefore, I ensured I brought the double stroller for Aaron and Abi. We decided to walk past the plaza in pursuit of the parade instead of waiting for it. We spent most of the night with Mari Carmen, Edu and their entire family. The parade began with large insect statues, wonderfully crafted to perfection. This frightened some children and excited others. My children were a little frightened at first. Then came large animals, from the lion to the deer. Each animal was filled with air, moving realistically with the wind. Some looked real and others fake, yet the craftsmanship in each was fantastic. We then began to see floats filled with children dressed like angels, cartoon characters, and soccer team members—every float possessing its unique and fun theme. The children laughed, screamed and jumped after every gift and candy thrown. Amari and D'iona ran through the streets until one in the morning chasing the parade collecting treats and gifts. Yet, to my surprise the parents, teens and young adults were doing the same. When it reached past one o'clock as the children became tired, we all called it a night. I have been to many parades in my lifetime growing up in America, but I have never seen a parade this beautiful. Every aspect of this parade was vibrant, professional and full of lights, colors, decor and music. The types of gifts that were thrown were very valuable, ranging from school supplies, book bags and candy, to T-shirts, toys, and jewelry. As the night came to an end, I felt slightly saddened yet grateful to have the opportunity to view and enjoy such a pleasurable endeavor with my children. This was definitely a sight to see and my family and I looked forward to the next year's parade.

While I do like spending time with my Spanish friends and enjoying their culture with them, it is also necessary for me to make time for my American friends as we partake in our own culture. I missed taking a day to myself with my friends to talk, laugh and pamper ourselves. Before I could ask, Jennifer read my mind and invited me for a ladies' day at a spa. I was delighted as well as excited because it has been a while since I received this form of treatment. Jennifer made an appointment for us both at eleven in the morning sharp. She signed me up for a facial, and a body massage for herself. I was very appreciative of Jennifer because a facial was much needed for me at the time.

Ana was the name of the aesthetician who performed my facial. Ana seemed to be very shy. She spoke very little English, but I could tell that she understood a lot more than she spoke. When she spoke, she would slow down her Spanish so I could understand, which was very considerate. I found her extremely intriguing because to my discernment, Ana possessed spiritual gifts she was unaware of. I also felt her kindred spirit of discernment. Having a profession that entails touching one's skin can be very intimate, in my opinion. For this reason, I felt a strong sense that Ana was able to read all of her clients' energy while giving them massages because this act of soothing the body relaxes most people. When a person is relaxed, they become more open. Curious, I asked Ana if she could. She looked at my phone as I translated the question. She then answered with a yes. I was not sure if Ana understood exactly what I was asking, but I was confident she comprehended enough. I was greatly appreciative of Ana's professionalism and kind heart. After our services were completed, we paid at the front desk as we said goodbye to the ladies. I was surprised at the price of a facial and understood that this was common. One of my greatest pros living in this country is the cheaper cost of services like facials, home improvements, car service and more. Many amenities like these are overpriced in the United States, which makes it difficult to prioritize. This mentality is not of Spain and for that I applaud this country.

    During the time that I have lived in Spain I have met people from all around the world. From Africa to Paris to South America. Each person I met had a different story to tell about their experience here in Spain—how they arrived and why they are here. For instance, there are free language classes held here in town. Zipporah wanted to improve her Spanish, so she started a Spanish course at an academy nearby. I did not possess the time or interest to attend this class until Zipporah invited me to their foreign exchange event. I was reluctant to go because I am more of a kinesthetic learner; I prefer to learn the language by socializing and talking with others. Nonetheless, I was glad that I agreed to attend the event with Zipporah because we met new people and the experience was pleasant. I exchanged numbers with this beautiful older melanated woman, and she informed me that she is a nurse. She cradled my face as if I were her daughter. I also met a beautiful, tall, and strong woman from Congo. She was proud and spoke French as well as a little English. She assisted Zipporah and me with our French speaking throughout the duration of the event. She openly expressed that she was interested in learning more English. It is always beautiful to witness and experience the exchanging of so many different people, languages and cultures all in one place. The event was hosted at the academy with all classes combined, Spanish, French and English. We met other women from Morocco, Portugal and Paris. Each participant was eager to enjoy the evening. The instructor broke everyone up into groups, ensuring each group was mixed with different languages. This gave each student an opportunity to practice the small phrases given to us by the instructor, in each language. Although I was opposed to attending the evening classes, I soon realized that it was an honor to be at this particular affair. I was cheerful that Zipporah invited me, and I learned a lot in that one evening.

    I bragged about the event to my friend Anastasia, the next morning and she informed me that many towns possess academies that offer free services as these. I was not only impressed to hear this, but I was equally enthused to know that these services existed free of charge. I can recall the deep conversation I began to have with my beautiful friend Anastasia, who is African in origin but adopted by a Spanish family. She grew up in Utrera, and her experiences living in Spain were mostly pleasant. She was raised by an incredible loving family. However, we both commonly shared likes and dislikes. She expressed her preference for the word "Negro/Negrita." I was stunned when I heard these words leave her mouth. Yet I also understood her perspective. This particular subject is not always easy to have with others who do not share the same feeling. Therefore, I do not often discuss this subject with others. However, I have mixed feelings about the words "Negro" or "black." Fifty percent of me has been conditioned to accept this word and identity since I was a child. Therefore, part of me embraces it and I am not always offended by it. I even sometimes refer to myself or my people as "black" with much pride. Yet, the fact remains that I am not the color black; therefore, being referred to as a "Negrita" or "Negra" would be a false assessment and description of who I am. I am a woman with melanin. I believe that labels carry great power. They can describe and/or create a negative or positive social identity. Some can form hostility throughout a community or group. In this case, the word "black," used to describe a group of people, has surely brought out hostility in the hearts of the modern African American, while others are honored to be black. Many even prefer to be called Black American versus African American. In my history being called black by Europeans was said to belittle the Africans brought over to America to become slaves. During these times, Europeans did not consider the African to be human; therefore, they began to recognize us as objects. Vava Tampa, an author and activist from Congo wrote in his article that "Africans had to be dehumanized in European society to facilitate their enslavement, colonization and exploitation of their land; hence the label 'black' because calling them African (or in their Yoruba, Benga, Shanti, Igbo,

Mandinka or Kongo names) recognizes their humanity, history, culture and heritage." I agree with this passage and am sometimes saddened by the poor habits passed down from generation to generation, which has become the norm. Yet, Anastacia and I both agreed that we chose to embrace the word "black" and use it with pride. We finished our conversation with laughter and joy. For we both admitted that no matter what we are called by other people, to us we will always be royal. Racism and discrimination have always been a battle for my people living in America. Many Black Americans even fear for their lives each and every day. From the wrongful treatments in society to the constant police brutality, it was never easy growing up as a brown child. However, moving to Spain has enlightened me in this subject. Although Spaniards are European and share a similar history with the American European, they are not the same. The energy toward people of color is different in Spain than back in the United States. While at the same time, some people are the same. A perfect instance of the difference is when Amos was pulled over by police officers in Utrera. This particular evening was during the communion season where many of the people participate in communion. Because of communion, many people celebrate; drinking, dancing and honoring their tradition. This evening, Amos was eager to come home because our family planned a nice weekend trip to Cadiz on the beach. Amos noticed that the traffic was backed up and he could see multiple police vehicles. He then realized that it was a standard checking point. As his car slowed down and he pulled up to the checkpoint, Amos observed about five police officers—all five fully armed. Two of the officers had full-size rifles. They all looked serious. One of the police approached Amos's car and asked for identification. The other officer stayed in the background while another officer with a rifle remained within eyesight range. He looked intimidating and ready to move if needed. The other officer asked my husband a few questions. Once the officer felt satisfied and comfortable, he politely told Amos to have a good day and Amos slowly drove off. This particular encounter gave Amos a better perspective on the difference between a Black American man being pulled over by police in Spain versus being a black man pulled over by cops in America. He envisioned how he probably would have felt nervous and fearful if that were to happen back in our country. Unfortunately, there are countless negative assumptions of people of color in the United States and all around the world. As a result, many people of color—men, women and children—have unjustly lost their lives, due to prejudgment, discrimination, and hate. I'm not claiming that all American police officers are bad. In fact, Amos's older brother is a proud police officer for the Dallas Police Department in Texas. However, many have the wrong motive and abuse their privileges as protectors of the law. This is the sad truth that has caused many black mothers and fathers to brief our children on how to deal with a cop. This conversation can be tough to have with a child. Some families from America feel obliged to flee the country and find a safer environment. I believe this experience with the Spanish cops made me and Amos even more appreciative of our lives here in Spain.

Most of my circumstances in Spain have been positive and some have not. At times I feel overwhelmed and dejected knowing that some things are out of my control. I enjoy my life as I watch my children grow and speak a different language. I am beyond grateful to have good friends and a daily routine that involves much excitement. Even so, some days I lack the desire to be around other people. For instance, one evening the children were invited to another birthday party. On this certain day I wanted to be alone and unbothered. However, as a mother of four active children, I am required to place their needs before mine. This birthday party was hosted at Illusionland. Only Aaron and Amari were to attend while D'iona and Abi stayed with me. Due to our family only owning one car, I was forced to find a ride. As we waited with Stella, I began to feel anxious and annoyed, yet I appreciated Stella for finding us a ride. Suddenly an unknown car pulled up and I comprehended that this woman was Stella's friend. The woman seemed nervous and did not speak much to us. I was relieved because I was already in a sour mood. She dropped off the boys and we headed to Burger King to meet the other mothers. When we arrived, I saw many new faces that I did not recognize. I could feel my spirit irking to leave. I wanted this evening to soon be over. I sat next to Conso A. and Mari Carmen. This group of women mostly consisted of friends of Mari Carmen and Conso A. These were friends I had not met until this day. The responses I received from the friends was that of intrigue yet discomfort and apprehension. This did not offend me because my family and I have become acquainted with this type of reaction when meeting new people here. Although I was not in the mood to eat or socialize, I did so. I ordered and quietly ate at the table with Stella, Conso A. and Mari Carmen, speaking very little. I enjoyed watching D'iona and Tere's older daughter Maria playing and bonding. They even played with Abi and watched her while I ate with the ladies. I realized that this was a challenging day and I needed to be recharged. I will always be thankful for my life's transformation from America to Spain. Yet, there are days where I feel disconnected and out of place while living here. There are moments when I miss being in the United States and moments that show me why I am not. Throughout every encounter in Utrera I have learned, grown and evolved as a person, a mother, a wife and a friend. I never take for granted the help I receive from my friends and from my family. I love being a mother and watching my children relish their new lives in a different country. I have fun becoming involved with the many school activities and events held each year.

Time was moving fast and the end of the school year was just around the corner. As a parent of Aaron's class, I was preparing for a big play performed at the end of each year. Some parents of each class were asked to play a role and find time to rehearse together. You see, at the end of every school year, the parents volunteer to perform different plays for our younger children. Each play is then displayed during school hours in the auditorium of the school. The children love these plays as they watch their parents become like children on stage. This year Aaron's class chose to perform a play about emotions. Each parent reenacted a particular emotion. In order to ensure everyone knew their roles, mandatory rehearsals were held. I specifically remember one particular rehearsal at Maria José's house. She did her best to encourage all of the busy parents to come. I admired her drive and passion. Many of the parents came, and some did not. María José and her husband, Alexander, lived in

Los Morales, which is about a seven- to ten-minute drive from Utrera. My neighbor, Vanessa was kind enough to give me a ride. We all met in their enormous garage, which they seemed to have reformed into a large entertainment space. Placed in the center of the garage was a large conference table. There was a small kitchen to the right and a nice bathroom in the back. I was already adoring the organization and hospitality before I even sat down. The parents all stood around and talked as we waited for others to arrive. Many of the parents sipped on coffee as María José and Ángeles made chocolate. Suddenly Alexander walks in with a large bag of churros. Everyone looked in excitement, for this was a popular and favorite snack in Spain. We all ate churros with chocolate as we waited for two more parents to arrive.

"Joy! Eat! Eat!" Anita demanded as she graciously shoved a churro into my mouth.

I was surprised but amused because I noticed that force-feeding and/or drinking was a common action here. When the churro entered my mouth, I felt a burst of bliss. The hot chocolate was sweet and creamy, while the churro was soft on the inside and crunchy on the outside. I truly enjoyed this snack and understood why it was so popular in Spain.

Finally, we began our rehearsal. We went through the entire play and danced a few times before everyone wanted to take a break. Many of the parents drank coffee prior because spending a Sunday afternoon rehearsing was a sacrifice. Other parents were tired and ready to leave. Suddenly I could see Maria José rushing out of the garage with her keys and purse in hand.

"María José! Where are you going?" one of the mothers passionately asked.

"I'm going to buy refreshments!" Maria announced with slight frustration in her voice.

My assumption was that her frustration stemmed from the desire to be a good host. She was limited on supplies as many stores were closed on Sundays. As a Spanish woman, her pride was slightly bruised, and she was on a mission to restore it. María José came back within five minutes carrying about five bottles of one-liter Cruzcampo beer and three large bags of chips. She quickly pulled out her nice glasses and before I could blink, every person had a glass of beer in their hands. After about ten minutes everyone seemed to be in a lighter and happier mood. We were all able to get a few more rehearsals done. This incident tickled me because I observed how the beer played as an expresso for the parents. We all had one glass and it was like the "magic potion" that brought everyone together. This made me realize why beer is so popular in the Spanish culture. It wasn't about the alcohol. It was about the socialization and fellowship. One of the parents informed me that Cruzcampo is one of the most popular brands of beers in Andalusia, Spain. However, my personal favorite is Estrella Galicia.

Ultimately, as the afternoon came to an end everyone began to help clean up. As most of the parents left, some of us stayed behind to socialize. Alexander, Loli and I conversed about Spanish olive oil. Together, they explained to me how olives are a large representation of Spain. They admitted that many people think the best olive oils are made in Italy. But, according to Alexander, Spain is one of the largest olive oil distributors in the world. This made perfect sense, as I recalled passing many olive fields in Andalusia. I always enjoy conversing with Spaniards because they were always open and willing to share their culture and history with me.

When I arrived home, I was happy to share my experience with Amos as we sat outside. The evening was beautiful as the sun started to set. The night arrived and so did the young teens. I liked how these young teens possessed the freedom to enjoy their friendships and connections with each other. However, I despised their lack of respect for their surroundings and in general. I continuously observed how the older women would weekly or sometimes daily clean their yards and part of the sidewalks. They take much pride and care in their homes and its cleanliness. Therefore, it bothered me to see how the young people combatted this cleanliness. Sitting outside I could hear many children and teens screaming to the top of their lungs and being disruptive. Many would have snacks, drinks and other disposable things. Each morning when I would walk my children to school, I could see the evidence of their gatherings. It annoyed me how many children and teens lacked regard for the earth. Throwing trash onto the ground. I also hated the fact that many of them are ignorant and miseducated on cultural things. They listen to hip-hop and think that it's OK to use the "N-word." They use it among themselves as if it is a fad, lacking the knowledge that this word carries so much hatred and pain and should *never* be uttered out of their mouths. Still, there are many young teens and children who display respect and are kind.

One particular evening I heard our doorbell ring. Not expecting company, I was puzzled as to who it could be. When I opened the gate, I was surprised to see a group of young boys and girls all dressed nicely. They asked for D'iona. I was glad to see D'iona making friends and being invited out. I allowed D'iona to go out with this group because I knew they were all good kids; unlike the groups I hear almost every night. D'iona came back that night cheerful, sharing with us the events of their affair. This became a regular routine for Amari and D'iona as I was happy to allow them to encounter things that I did not have the privilege of doing as a child. As a child growing up, I was deprived of many escapades and my father raised my siblings and me extremely religious. Our youth consisted of church, school, and home. Although I did have a fairly good life as a child, I felt grateful that my children could experience the same things that I did growing up and more.

Even though my younger days consisted of mostly church functions, I did enjoy the many festivities, especially Easter Sunday. Here in Spain their *Semana Santa* is celebrated differently than Easter Sundays celebrated in the United States. One of the largest differences is the religious processions of Spain. This particular week many processions were held. During a school night, my sister and I decided to attend the procession with Maria and Danny. I was determined to view and experience this particular procession. Many of my local friends informed Zipporah and me that during Holy Week, the *Procesión de los Pasos* was the most important, the crucifix of Christ. As a Black American, non-Catholic Christian woman, my observation of this particular tradition in Spain may be offensive for some and understandable to others. Nonetheless, I must be honest about my personal perception. I've observed that Spaniards are extremely traditional and serious about their religion, which is primarily Catholicism. As I viewed the procession, I was reminded of the differences in our culture. When I walk into a Catholic church, my primary observation is the many statues of Christ hanging on a cross. Growing up, my father and mother taught us to never possess a cross with Christ on it. Our parents felt that having a cross with Christ on it emphasized his crucifixion too much, and not His resurrection enough. As I became older, I understood this. As a child the image of Christ dead on a cross would taunt me.

    Stella later explained to me how each part of Spain celebrated differently. For example, Andalusia chose to remember Christ's crucifixion. Therefore, their processions display just that. I saw intense and vivid imagery of Jesus on the cross as his mother Mary mourned in tears beneath him. The procession was beautifully crafted, making the scene look real. I felt a slight sense of guilt for having spectated this viewing in brief admiration. I commend and respect the dedication that every participant displayed as they seemed to have planned for the processions six to twelve months in advance; from the musicians to the little children. They took pride in their roles, apparel and jobs. The men came together to carry the gold statue of Jesus on the cross, weighing thousands of pounds. As I researched the history of Spain's processions, I read that the *costaleros* (float bearers), consisting of twenty-four to forty-eight volunteers, are hidden inside the platform of the *paso*, which makes it appear to be moving on its own. I have learned that historically, dock workers were hired to carry the pasos. However, after 1973, the task was universally taken over by the members of the confraternities that organize each procession. Only members of this particular organization were permitted to carry the platform. Each member was mandated to wear purple cloaks with matching hoods made from fine silk. This troubled me when I first saw it because their attire is very similar to the attire of the Ku Klux Klan, a brutally racist group that haunts the history of Black Americans. I could see many feet under the statute, all different shapes and sizes, the weight of the statue causing much pressure on their legs and feet. All spectators including the children clapped in favor and appreciation for the volunteers. It was as though we were attending a funeral. People dressed nicely following the procession down the streets of the town, some crying with heads hanging low. The music was somber along with the drums pounding slowly to the rhythm of the procession. Meanwhile, in the Black American culture, we focus on the resurrection of Christ. We commemorate how Christ defeated death by rising back to life on the third day. For our Easter Sunday, we gather at the church dressed in our finest clothing, consisting of floral designs and many colors. Primarily purple or lavender to symbolize the penance, humility, and sorrow of Jesus Christ's suffering. The sermon for that day derived from this knowledge, that Christ died yet rose on the third day. Our energy is always happy and hyper, and everyone shouts and dances in appreciation for Christ's sacrifice. In Spain, their procession began with a vivid image of Christ hung to the cross in agony. It would then end in a local cemetery. Everything seemed to be focused on the death of Christ. Nonetheless, the homage and dedication are admirable. As a musician I enjoyed the live daunting yet beautiful music during each procession. The sound of the trumpets echoing throughout the entire town of Utrera gave me chills. Many thoughts ran through my mind as Zipporah and I headed home. Like me, Zipporah enjoyed the night with Maria and Danny, yet disliked the realistic image of Christ hanging from the cross. It brought us back to the death of our own mother, which made us both despondent. This helped me to realize why it is more important to celebrate his rising rather than to commemorate his death. Nonetheless, this is an important tradition for the country of Spain.

Spain's annual feria (fair) is also an important tradition of Spain, which is by far one of my favorite traditional experiences here. My family and I bask in the grand gestures and excitement of this celebration. Each town and/or city has its own feria held at different times throughout the year. The Feria of Utrera is held annually during the first week of September from the 4th to the 8th. I believe they chose the best season of the year to have a fair that is primarily hosted outside. The sun is shining, yet the sky is fresh and clear, while the breeze is chilled and crisp. I equally enjoy it being held one to two weeks before school starts for the children. What I have gathered about the feria tradition in Spain is that there are two important aspects of the feria. The first is the tradition and the second is religious. Anytime I wanted to gather true facts about Utrera, or even Spain, I would ask Mr. Carlos from my children's school. Mr. Carlos took pride in elaborating and explaining the facts of his town and country. I wanted to know more about its significance. How did this amazing event come to pass, and when? I contacted the right person because Mr. Carlos made it clear to me, which helped my family and me to enjoy this formal bash even more. He informed me that in Spanish, as in English, the word feria has several meanings. *Una feria* is an exhibition or a fair. For example, a book fair or an art fair. These fairs are organized specifically to show or sell things. Besides that, una feria can also be a festival or an amusement park. I enjoyed how he began with the origin of the word *feria* because when I first heard about the fair from Tina, my mind instantly thought of the fair I would attend annually as a child. This fair consisted of rides, food, many attractions live and fake. Yet, with the knowledge from Mr. Carlos, I realize that the fair I attended as a child is considered "una feria." He brought to my attention that Utrera's feria began as a fair for trading. As years passed, the trade fair evolved into a large festival. He expounded on the history as if it was his own childhood history. This gave me the religious aspect of the feria. Mr. Carlos explained that "around the middle of the sixteenth century, in the place where today is El Santuario de Consolación, there was a little hermitage or chapel with the image of La Virgen de Consolación. This image had a reputation of being very miraculous."

I personally knew this to be true because I have become accustomed to seeing these many images on the walls of many homes. For example, a beautiful, marbled painting is arrayed on the patio of Zipporah's house. He continued to explain with precise detail.

"The strategic location of Utrera, which is between Cádiz, Sevilla and Málaga, made Utrera a common place to stop while traveling. The big bustle and activity in the area related to the travels and trade with America, the New World. These enterprises caused Utrera to become a very important religious center on a national level. Utrera also became an important pilgrimage point. This important concentration of people would usually occur every year, around the 8th of September, the day of the festivity of La Virgen de Consolación. Many stalls, traders, adventurers, cattle breeders, and more would settle down and rest around this chapel in Utrera, giving thanks and paying respect for their earnings. The fame of Utrera's fair and pilgrimage grew until, for political reasons, a king, Carlos III, banned it. However, the devotion to La Virgen de Consolación has continued until our days. Presently the feria is a very important popular festival that takes place every year on or around the 8th of September."

After hearing Mr. Carlos's detailed exposition, I could feel his pride in my heart through every word. Goosebumps ran down the skin of my arms and I instantly imagined myself at the feria in the sixteenth century. I imagined the attire then, compared to the immaculate attire now: polka dot dresses, floral hats, large fans and more.

How did they dress then? I asked myself while getting dressed for my second feria. The first year was a trial year for my family and me, not just for the feria, but for all of the many events of the year. Therefore, we were not sure as to how to dress or what to expect. Nonetheless, I could already visualize my entire family in the traditional attire, as I walked through the fair the first night with Mariali. I consciously made a decision that I wanted my family and me to honor the tradition with our attire at the following year's event. We were going to look amazing. Meanwhile, this year Mariali and I decided to meet for the first night with our children. It was astonishing watching the millions of lights flicker throughout the night as our children ran and played under the stars. They rode on almost every ride, ate as much candy as they pleased, as well as played the many games available. I could not believe my eyes when I saw the full completion of the feria. Each corner of the fairground was covered in decorations, tents sky-high accompanied with bars in each one. The rides were loud, cheerful and full of colors. The sky was lit with every color of fireworks. I was convinced that the people surely took pride in this event, with every man dressed in his best suit, while the women looked like flamenco dolls perfectly adorned and decorated. I was almost embarrassed to be dressed so plainly, but I was not alone. There were people from all around Andalusia, foreign and non-foreign. Most knew the tradition, and some did not. Nevertheless, everyone was having a grand time. Mariali and I talked and smiled at the joy of our children playing.

The second night of the feria was only the adults. Amos and I walked to meet with Zipporah and a group of our friends. As my husband and I walked to the feria, I was overwhelmed with emotion. The beauty of the enriched culture of this country filled my heart. There were so many people attending on Saturday night! Families dressed in traditional flamenco attire, embracing the pride of who they are and what the feria meant for their town's history. It was absolutely splendid, for it was an experience that I did not want to take for granted. The moon was at its waning crescent phase, which gave less light to the night. Yet, it was not needed during these past few nights, for the festival handled that job. The wind was light yet freshly brisk as people's spirits were high. The feria for Spaniards seemed to be a place where time stood still for five days and nights as all worries diminished (if only for that short while). They enjoyed their time with their friends and family, eating, singing, dancing, drinking, and overall preserving their culture—something that can only be described once experienced—lights, music, horses, flamenco attire, laughter, singing, and so on. These sounds reigned the streets of Utrera as my family and I joined in the festivities. After walking and exploring all night we ran into Tina and her closest friends. They invited us to a *caseta* to see Alfonso perform. A caseta is a tent at the feria where either food, drinks or entertainment is being served. Some entries are free while others are private. One would only enter a private caseta if invited and we were honored to receive this invitation. This particular caseta possessed more of an antique theme. The decor was lavish and rich. The people were welcoming and happy. Alfonso's performance was awesome as he and his band sang their hearts out. The keyboardist played like he was Latino in origin. The guitarist was very talented in his traditional flamenco skills. The percussionist had a rhythm that can only be learned through culture. Alfonso is a true performer! He sings for enjoyment but knows exactly how to keep the crowd going. He showed great musicianship as he knew how to transition his band. He sang beautifully even though I did not understand all of the words; I was moved by the passion and great showmanship. The way in which Spaniards sing is unlike any other people in the world. It is almost like a combination of Arabic singing, blues and gospel. By the end of his performance Alfonso was extremely fatigued but he continued to sing as the crowd pleaded for more.

"OTHER! OTHER!" the crowd chanted in unison. I could see he was tired, but I knew he and his band had a bit more life to give. Everyone clapped and screamed in delight as they began another song at everyone's request. I could gauge that the musicians equally seemed to be enjoying themselves. Everyone sang together like a choir as if the song performed was everyone's favorite in the caseta. Alfonso kept the crowd entertained with his alluring voice as everyone danced and sang along. My family and I could not believe the fun we had on both nights. We all reminisced about the feria for months, planning for the next year ahead. Listed below are my ten favorite things about Spain:

1. Culture of Andalusia: Very traditional. They hold on to their customs and traditions.
2. The importance of FAMILY.
3. The flamenco culture: It is similar to African and black American church music rhythm. From the hand clapping to the foot stomping of passionate movements and singing.
4. Cadiz beaches: There are so many different coastal beaches throughout the province of Cadiz, but they are all unique and beautiful in their own way.
5. Architecture: Historical and beautiful. Additionally, seeing the Moorish influence in some of the architecture.
6. Estrella Galicia Beer: It's one of the leading beers of Spain. It's not too strong and slightly sweet.

7. Bidet: These are lower toilets with no tops that are used to clean private areas after using the restroom. I absolutely love the convenience of these and cannot believe I lived all these years without it!
8. The fresh foods, fruits and vegetables in the local fruit stores. As well as the store "Mercadona." The food is fresh, and the stores are everywhere! It's like a Spanish version of Publix in America.
9. The rum "Negrita." This quickly became Zipporah's and my favorite drink. The name and picture changed my perspective as it pertains to being addressed as a "young black woman".
10. The Queen of Spain, Letizia, and her influence to change Spain's ancient perspective of women and women's rights. As well as her two beautiful daughters, who in my eyes are a representation of my own young daughter, Abi.

Chapter 5:

Exploring Spain

I would have to admit to the world that my travels through Spain have been my most joyous moments—from Seville to Marbella, from Barcelona to Madrid and many more cities. Within the past two and a half years, my family and I have traveled a tremendous amount compared to the times we've traveled in the States. I can remember discussing with Amos before the move, how important it was that we travel as a tribe and explore the land we have decided to call home. As we first arrived in Utrera, Spain, there was one task I wanted us to complete together before settling in. I wanted us to develop goals for ourselves. Therefore, one beautiful morning, Amos, Zipporah, the children and I all created a "dream sheet." On this sheet we were all permitted to write down the goals we wanted to set for our lives in Spain. It was adorable watching Aaron and Abi write out their goals with crayon, not sure of the power within their words. After everyone finalized their sheets—including goals set for the first month, first six months, the first year, and ending with the first five years—everyone was asked to read them out loud. This idea stemmed from my favorite writer of all time, Toni Morrison. Her writing explores the identity of blacks in America. Reading her books would often force me into her mind, visualizing every word written, feeling all emotions. This was an idea I gathered from taking her advice. Toni Morrison advised all of her readers to "use the world around you." I know in my heart that writing the words then speaking them is a way of developing our foundation of faith. I could envision the trips we would take throughout the year, viewing monuments, experiencing various events, meeting new people, and eating exotic foods. I wanted to ensure I not only use the world around me, but in doing so, I wanted to share that world by exposing our lives here in Spain. After we all read our "dream sheets," I noticed something we all shared in common. We all wanted to travel more.

Marbella was our family's first vacation in Spain. For that particular reason, Amos, Zipporah and I decided to make this trip spectacular. Not only was this trip for our immediate family, but one of my oldest and best friends, Sophie, and her eight-year-old son (and our godson), Elijah, joined us all the way from Hungary. Amos and I met Sophia during our first years in the United States Air Force, as young airmen. We laughed as we reminisced about the past. We also invited our closest family friends here in Spain, Tina and her family. However, only Tina and her mother, Tia Patri, were able to accompany us on this first trip. Although it was early November and a little chilly, we knew that we wanted to be near the ocean. Being near the ocean was important to us because it reminded us of being back home in South Florida. We found an amazing large house for two to three nights directly in front of a well-known beach called Playa de la Venus. Marbella is a beautiful, popular urban city located on the southern coast of Andalusia, Spain. It has many beaches stretching far and wide along its coast. The beauty of the photos on the site was immaculate and the reviews were all convincing. Everyone was excited and ready to commence this trip to a city we have heard a lot about. The home was like a mansion. It was large with many upgrades. The floors were all laid with marble, the furniture modernized, and the pool was crystal clear. It accommodated three different families and the price was a steal. We hit the jackpot and found the perfect stay for our first vacation. Sophia and Elijah were in town for four days; therefore, we wanted to ensure this would be a trip they would never forget. They arrived in Seville on a late Wednesday evening and were scheduled to return to Hungary on that following Sunday afternoon. The first night we all spent time at home in Utrera, catching up on old memories and settling Sophia and Elijah in. The next evening Tina invited Zipporah, Sophia and me to a gathering at Cristina and Pablo's country family home. We ate snacks, danced, laughed, and played games we have never played before. It was an interesting night and Sophia seemed to have had a great time.

We rented an extra vehicle and left early Friday afternoon for Marbella. It was a three-and-a-half-hour drive. Zipporah drove the rental car—a Mercedes Benz with Sophia, Tina, and Tia Patri, while my family and I were in our larger van. The scenery was amazing as we drove up and down many mountains, crossing through various alluring lands. I did not hesitate to retrieve my camera to record the beauty of God's creation. It was a perfect three-and-a-half-hour ride through the south of Spain. The moment we arrived at Marbella, we encountered a problem finding the home. This city was tremendously different from Utrera and Seville and the streets were very confusing. An hour passed and the children began to become agitated. Consequently, we did not find the home until around six thirty that evening. Everyone was frustrated, tired and hungry. Nevertheless, we all arrived safely and were anxious to enter the home. When we first stepped into the house all of our negative feelings dissipated. The home was simply magnificent. It was grand, elegant and modern, as stated on the website. Every one of us was in awe at the charm of the home. The host kindly showed us around and gave us a short briefing about the house and its perks. We were all so enthused and grateful. We all seemed to embody a sense of gratitude and merriment to have all arrived in one piece. I could feel chills in my body, thinking of the many obstacles my family and I endured before making this journey to Spain. Afterward, we all had dinner, played with the children, then relaxed. The house had six large bedrooms with five bathrooms, a large black and white upgraded kitchen, and a dining area suitable for all parties. When we ventured outside, we were greeted with much vegetation, two sparkling pools and a breathtaking landscape. The backyard had multiple gardens all covered in colorful flowers, bright green grass and tall palm trees. There were two bedrooms with two restrooms on the main floor, furnished for two persons in each room. Upstairs was a master suite and a mini-suite. Both were well designed with large private restrooms. Meanwhile, the master bedroom possessed a large terrace overlooking the backyard with a lovely view of the ocean. There was even a smaller room with a restroom off the side of the kitchen down in the basement. This room remained vacant, but it was nice to know it was available. All of the flooring throughout the entire house was a light grey colored marble and insulated. After settling in the home that night, we allowed the children to watch cartoons on the large flat-screen television in the living room. Tia Patri sat with the children as they all drifted asleep in the comfortable sofas. Zipporah, Sophia, Amos, Tina and I sat in the yard to recoup and socialize. We danced, talked and laughed all night. But, due to the long journey prior, we all began to feel sleepy and exhausted. We all said our good nights and went our separate ways to sleep.

The next morning, Amos, Tia Patri and Tina went to Mercadona to purchase groceries. When they returned Amos quickly cooked up a mouthwatering breakfast: potatoes, eggs, and vegetables with biscuits. We all ate breakfast together as a unit in the large dining area. During the day we relaxed as we searched online to find something to do for the children. Later in the evening we decided to explore the city of Marbella. We went to the center of the town and did a little shopping. The malls were enormous with every store a person could think of. The children had a blast walking through the toy store. We allowed them all to pick one big toy for themselves. Along our walk we discovered a small neighborhood fair. The children jumped on a trampoline, rode in electric cars and played arcade games. We, the adults, did not hesitate to join the children in this fun. We played tag, rode the cars as well and took many photos. As the area began to close and the nightlife started, we knew it was time to get our little ones in the house and ready for bed. Everyone had a fulfilling and eventful day. Later that night, Zipporah, Sophie and I went out dancing. We tried to get Tina to come along but she was too tired. Therefore, the three of us caught a cab and went to the club. We got tipsy, danced, laughed, walked around, and met different people. We ended up at a Russian karaoke bar and met three black men. I remember having an inspirational conversation with them about the consciousness of our people. One of the men we met at the Russian bar was from Jamaica. He was middle-aged, bald with a salt-and-pepper colored beard. He was nicely dressed and was confident yet humble. He performed "No Woman, No Cry" and sounded like a professional reggae artist. He was extremely handsome and intelligent. He seemed to be spiritually conscious in my opinion. There was also a younger man who slightly resembled the middle-aged man. He was from the Virgin Islands and also intelligently charming. The third man was from Senegal, also young, handsome and kind. His name was Moses. He was young but married with two children.

As we exited this Russian karaoke bar, we were approached by two intoxicated Spanish men who addressed Moses in a disrespectful way. Zipporah instantly defended Moses with aggression and passion.

"Don't speak to this man that way! He's a king!" she yelled at them. Moses smiled with pride and joined Zipporah in chastising these ignorant and drunk men.

"Yes! And these women are queens!" he yelled as he grabbed his bike.

Over the past few years, black people throughout the world have begun to address themselves as fellow "queens and kings," representing our royal lineage as well as encouragement, love and respect toward one another. We spoke a little about where we were all from and why we were in Spain. When I glanced over my shoulder, I could see a look of confusion and embarrassment on the faces of those men. This made me smile inside as I was proud of my sister and Moses for defending themselves. Young Moses rode into the night on his bike with a smile on his face as we walked down the street, exploring the area with a smile on ours. As we continued to walk, searching for food and a different club, we all laughed about the last incident. We finally stopped at a disco that was playing good music. We wanted to enter, but the security seemed to have an issue. I could not understand him entirely, but I think he had an issue with our casual attire. Suddenly, two drunk European men attempted to greet and address us using the N-word. We all looked at one another in disbelief. Zipporah quickly corrected him and advised him to never use that word again. Meanwhile, the bouncer turned to his colleague to ask if it was OK for us to enter. With my bionic ears, I heard what I perceived to be disrespectful verbiage.

"Excuse me, are you speaking about us?" I quickly interrogated in Spanish.

They both looked at me in surprise as I grinned at them in disapproval. The man stood there in his ignorance and shame with his jaw wide open. Surprised, embarrassed and confused he denied saying it. He asked if I knew Spanish and I told him that I was learning but knew enough. By this time, Zipporah and

Sophie's attention were redirected to my conversation with this bouncer. But Zipporah quickly ended it.

"Can we get in or not?" she asked with hostility.

Ashamed and exposed they let us in. Sophia insisted that he probably did in fact say it because he seemed too upset to be innocent. Not allowing the tackiness of this man to disturb our good vibes, we walked in with pride. We found a perfect place to dance and be to ourselves. It was a VIP spot and perfectly cozy for the three of us. We danced until we were too tired to stand. It was a blast.

"Girl! It's like your sister has a battery in her back! She just doesn't stop!" Sophie exclaimed.

We both laughed as I totally agreed. Zipporah is consistently the same when we go out dancing. Lively, fun and a serious dance machine. As the night began to come to an end, so did our energy. We called it a night and caught a cab safely back to the house.

Later that morning, we all had breakfast and packed up all our things. We wanted to make sure that Sophie and Elijah made it to the airport in Seville on time. Amos and I drove them to the airport, while Zipporah stayed with the children. It was a bittersweet moment saying our goodbyes to Sophia and Elijah, but I knew we would see each other again. We will all cherish this memory forever, because the trip to Marbella symbolized the time, hard work and sacrifice it took for my family and me to get to a point of pure life. Including my best friend Sophie.

As the winter approached so did the cold air. I have always enjoyed the winter times because of the holiday festivities. But the cold was not an aspect of the winter that I relished. Our first year in Spain was more of an introduction to the ways of the province. We learned their culture, traditions, ways of life and geography. One piece of information that stuck out in my mind was the knowledge of the Canary Islands. Months prior to making this move, I made it my purpose to inform myself about this country. The more I read about Spain, the more I discovered similarities between the United States. The Canary Islands reminded me of the five territory islands of the United States: American Samoa, Guam, the Northern Mariana Islands, Puerto Rico and the US Virgin Islands. It also made me think of the neighboring islands as well: the Bahamas, Jamaica, Haiti and more. Many of these islands exude beauty, nature and black pride. The Canary Islands interested me as did the islands of my own country.

It was a must for me to visit an island, if not all. Therefore, Zipporah and I decided to take a "sister trip" to one of those islands. We were both in accord with the decision as we instantly began searching for lodgings and flights. Although it was cold with a little rain, Zipporah and I were determined to make this trip our thrilling reality. Viewing all islands as we researched what each had to offer, Zipporah and I equally agreed on Lanzarote. The island was prepossessing in nature yet with an eerie aura. Perhaps the combination of the gloomy weather and dark sands is what formed my opinion. Either way, we enjoyed our entire stay there. We found a delightful Airbnb that overlooked the east side of the island's ocean. The host gave us great directions to the apartment. The ride from the small airport to this quaint town was spectacular. Zipporah and I gazed in amazement as the cab driver politely gave us a little history about the island. She asked about our place of origin and we asked about hers. Her music had Zipporah swaying back and forth. She never rejected a chance to dance. The cab driver and I chuckled at the sight of her bopping up and down to the beat. I believe we brought joyfulness and pride to this woman during this one-hour ride into town. This trip was very important to me and a much-needed vacation. As a mother of three, it can be difficult to find time alone. I had not undergone a trip without my children and husband in years. I was not only grateful to share this experience with my sister, but I was equally appreciative of Amos for honoring my wish and most importantly understanding the need for it. He drove us to the airport the morning of our trip and wished us both a great time.

Upon our arrival we were greeted by a kind man, our host. He showed us around the two-bedroom apartment and gave us much-needed information about the restaurants along with the many activities Lanzarote had to offer. The apartment was cozy and perfectly sized for two persons or four. The decor was teal with an artistic beach theme. All appliances were updated, and everything was clean. We were gifted a bottle of white wine as a warm welcome from the host. The man gave us the keys and left. Zipporah and I smiled at each other with a full heart as we began to settle in. After putting our things up and walking two steps to the market for groceries, we decided to take a stroll. We wanted to become acquainted with the town. There were many unique homes spread throughout the hills, mountains, and coastline. There were also a variety of seafood-based restaurants toward the end of the town. We stopped and ate at a nice outdoor restaurant where everything was delicious and fresh. We also met a young European couple who were also foreigners of Spain. They were awkwardly friendly yet reserved. They informed us that visiting the Canary Islands was an annual tradition for them as a couple. This information warmed my heart as I thought of my relationship goals with Amos. They assured us that Lanzarote is a breathtaking island.

My sister and I enjoyed our lunch, local wine and conversation as we laughed about our childhood past. Seeing that the east bank of the island was directly in front of us, we decided to ask about the ferry rides. The cashier was kind and spoke very good English. She gave us a schedule as well as explained it to us in clear detail. She was happy to entertain any questions we had about the trip as well as the island. She also took the time to assist us in finding the best activities on the island. Finally, we walked home and spent the rest of the night on the balcony, dancing, singing, and reminiscing as the sun set. The air was crisp and clear as the sky lit up in the most astonishing red and orange glow. We stayed up dancing and laughing, shooting videos with our phones as if we were creating a film. Night fell and the silence rocked us both to sleep. We both climbed into the king-size bed and went straight to sleep.

The next morning was cloudy with a high chance of rain. Nevertheless, that did not discourage Zipporah or me against exploring. We ate breakfast, got dressed and walked to the ferry nearby. We took a boat to another island called Graciosa where we would find excursions. The boat ride was tranquil, informative and smooth. We could see other islands as we slowly drifted on the water. The mountain views were astonishing. When we finally arrived at Graciosa we decided to walk around and explore before venturing on an excursion. After eating a small lunch, Zipporah and I both decided to take a five-mile biking expedition to the most famous beach of the Canaries called Playa de las Conchas. We rented fairly new mountain bikes from a local family-owned rental on the island, near the restaurant where we had lunch.

    As we began the journey, I observed the harsh terrain. The trail seemed a little rough and I was secretly nervous. The bike owners' young son along with his younger cousin, led us outside of the village. I was very impressed by their speed as they both ran ahead while Zipporah and I followed on our bikes. We patiently kept up, admiring their silence and stealth to get us on track. Once we exited outside of the village, we tipped the two children and headed to our destination. It put a smile on our faces as we watched them both receive the tip with much excitement. We coincidentally ran into the same nice European couple that we met the day before. They were on the same excursion but a different route and a different company. We all stayed close together knowing that none of us were secure in our sense of direction in this foreign land. The trail was rocky, the scenery was pleasant, and the clouds were getting fuller by the minute. Yet my sister and I were determined to get to the Playa de las Conchas, as was the couple nearby. We both wanted to take a dip into this particular ocean if for only a moment. About forty-five minutes later, we finally arrived at our destination and it was absolutely stunning. There were miles of open shore to the north side as well as pitch-black rocks with brown sand to the south. Many coves and caves had formed because of the strong water currents and rocks. With their own little pools of beaches, this island spoke volumes to our souls. It was simply amazing. It was windy and slightly cold as we were both perspiring from the long bike ride. Zipporah and I found the perfect spot, laid a towel onto the sand and offloaded our small backpacks. Looking around, there was literally no one in sight. With the exception of the European couple a long distance off, Zipporah and I were the only persons on this beach, so we took advantage. We both felt compelled to take at least one swim on this lovely Canary beach. Zipporah went first. She took every article of clothing off and fearlessly dove into the ocean naked. I silently spectated while reflecting on my life. A few minutes later, Zipporah returned and exclaimed how great the water felt. She elaborated on its shocking chill and the thrill of the waves hitting her body. Suddenly, it was my turn to take a dip. I slowly stood up in my one-piece bathing suit, watching the waves move back in forth with a strong force. I instantly thought of the scriptures of God, referring back to Job 12:7–10 where it states:

"But ask the animals, and they will teach you, or the birds in the sky, and they will tell you; or speak to the earth, and it will teach you, or let the fish in the sea inform you. Which of all these does not know that the hand of the LORD has done this? In his hand is the life of every creature and the breath of all mankind."

Pondering on these words I began to gaze at the birds in the sky, I observed the water's movement as I grounded my feet into the cool brown sand. I stared at the mountains from afar, breathing in the fresh air.

"You want me to come with you, sis?" Zipporah offered in support as she interrupted my thoughts and private mental prayer.

"No. I'm good," I quickly and calmly answered without hesitation.

I felt that I needed to do this alone. I walked toward the loud and crashing waves and just dove in. Completely submerged, I allowed for the waves to play toss with my body. I opened my eyes underneath the water as I always do. All I could see were bubbles with green and blue shades of water whooshing around my silhouette. It felt as if I were in another world. Finally, I emerged, inhaling and exhaling deeply as if I were a newborn taking my first breath into the world. Zipporah was right, the water did feel great! I relished in the ocean for a few more minutes then joined Zipporah on the shore. As we quietly sat there, I remember thinking how I would love to come back to this very beach during the best time of the summer—accompanied by the whole family. Swimming and sitting on that beach was more than just an excursion. It was a spiritual release for my sister and me. To let go of the hurt and pain of our past and embrace our peace and joy of our present and future.

We explored the rocks and caves for a little while and decided to head back in time to catch the evening ferry. It was windy and cloudy as the rain began to pour. Nevertheless, we pushed through the five miles back. Along our way we met a group of friendly young Europeans who were studying abroad. This trip was a dream come true for most of them, as well as for my sister and me. They all spoke English, expressing their passion for the Spanish language and culture. We conversed with them for most of the way back into the town, which helped pass the time. When we finally made it back to our Airbnb, we were both exhausted. We showered and Zipporah made a nice homemade dinner for us. Red pasta with fried mushrooms on top. It was delicious and right on time. That night was a repeat of the night before as we danced, sipped and listened to our favorite jams from a Soulection episode by our favorite DJ, Joe K. This trip to Lanzarote was not only monumental, but it was also a therapeutic getaway for me. My sister and I bonded more, opening our hearts and revealing more secrets to one another. We both gained more understanding and appreciation for each other. On our way back to Lanzarote Airport, we agreed that this needed to be an annual trip for us both. A special "sister trip" to get away, bond and let loose. Not only did Zipporah and I travel to the Canary Islands together, but we also made it our goal to travel to other cities and towns. I was happy to have my sister here with me. She was becoming another best friend.

 I am full of gratefulness when I think about the blessing of having my two best friends with me. My husband and my sister. While Amos is nonchalant, rational and logical, both I and Zipporah are just the opposite and we all balanced each other out. We made a great family team. Zipporah was always being invited to different events, parties, and trips and was not hesitant to invite Amos and me. She would often express to me how she missed home. But Spain was growing on her. She simply wished for a place that welcomed diversity, not just referring to people but also to cultures, traditions, entertainment, foods and more. My family and I possessed a strong desire to introduce our culture, lifestyle and traditions to Spain. Sharing our American ways while they share theirs. We decided to create a YouTube channel for our children called AG3 Kidz TV, highlighting multilingual education. This became a success and something that we all enjoyed together. However, Amos, my children and I are also musicians and we desired to integrate that aspect of our lives here in Spain as well. Yet, we also had to find those opportunities.

Zipporah was blessed with many gifts as well, and one of them is writing. Predominantly poetry. She was beginning to yearn for a way to exhibit her artistry of poetry. Soon after, she found a perfect opportunity to feed her yearning. However, this event was in Barcelona, which is about six hundred miles north of Utrera. But distance was not stopping my sister from fulfilling her dream of performing her spoken word in Spain.

Zipporah came into contact with a man who was hosting poetry slams at a bar called Tinto in Barcelona. These slams were held once a month and usually on a weekend. Zipporah felt this was her time. The event was created to encourage poets all around Spain to push past their norms and recite their poetry timed, with limited mistakes and in front of judges. Zipporah's heart was set on going and I desperately wanted to join her! I discussed the trip with Amos as we both agreed that I should be there to support my big sister. Zipporah and I saw this as an opportunity to welcome a "girls' trip." Zipporah invited Jessica and Tazjaa to join as well and they both obliged. Both Jessica and Tazjaa shared the same feeling as me. Pride. Not only was I excited about visiting Barcelona for the first time, but I was even more ecstatic about seeing my sister perform live for the first time at a competition! Both our lives led us directly to various unique places and experiences. This was one of them.

The best part about this journey was that it gave us both a chance to reconnect our sisterhood as adults. Growing up as children we were always very close. But we lost that closeness when our parents died, and everyone ventured in different directions to find themselves. On these voyages to self-awareness, my siblings and I realized that we needed one another. Consequently; we made it our duty to stay tethered.

Zipporah and I made a strategic plan with Jessica to have a memorable time in Barcelona. We purchased our flights, rented our stay and proceeded with the plan. We all took an early flight to Barcelona on Thursday morning. Tazjaa was scheduled to work on Thursday and promised to meet us there on Saturday. If only for one day, she wanted to see her friend perform live as well. We all did. Zipporah, Jessica and I walked around, exploring Barcelona for two days! The city is bursting with life and diversity. I personally have never seen so many Europeans with locs until I visited Barcelona. The people there were from all around the world, from tourists to citizens. They were all together living their exciting city lives. It was a thrilling sight to see. Various parts of Barcelona were populated with people from all around the world: Arabs, Turks, Chinese, and so on. The architecture was equally unique and stunning. The people seemed more carefree, confident and happy. Friday night we went to a club that was playing "Shackles" by Mary Mary. I found this to be extremely amusing that in 2019, a Black American Christian group was being played at a night club in Barcelona, Spain! We were so pleased with the work of the DJ. He played a wonderful variety of music, from pop to reggaeton to Afro beats and salsa. We met so many different people, including a group of young

African men who were beautiful and polite. We continued the night with laughter, talking and more foot tapping.

The next day Zipporah and Jessica decided to explore more of the city while I slept in. Tazjaa arrived later that afternoon. She settled in the third room as we both waited for Jessica and Zipporah to return. When they returned, they shared with us the amazing day they had. They walked up a hill to a distant natural garden, saw many monuments and fountains and even bought street art from a Cuban man. Zipporah cooked a tasty meal while we all made preparations for the event of the night. We all ate together at the table then got dressed. We navigated our way to Tinto bar and to our surprise it was only a three-minute walk which was perfect and convenient. We were greeted with smiles and positive vibes once we arrived.

This particular poetry organization created a warm space where poets could bare their hearts on the stage with no criticism or hatred. Although the poetry slam was a competition, it was equally an opportunity to express. All performances were permitted to be spoken in English. I was happy about that because I loved poetry and wanted to relax, not be worrying about trying to translate. The bar and stage were both rugged and chic. There was a total of nine participants and three judges. We met a kind woman where we sat. She was quirky and liberal. We all socialized before the slam began. She exclaimed that she was from Barcelona and even gave us all a little insight about the city. She spoke various languages, including Barcelona's own language called Catalán. It was interesting to know that Barcelona, along with other certain parts of Spain, speak Catalán as their primary language. Consequently, "most Barcelonans are multilingual," the young woman explained to us. I was appreciative of this conversation and so were Jessica, Tazjaa and Zipporah.

To our surprise, Zipporah was the only native English speaker competing. I believe this gave her an advantage along with the fact that she was a well-seasoned performer. The spoken word was not just a hobby for Zipporah, but a special gift God gave to her. I was confident that Zipporah could win this slam. Meanwhile, I was exceptionally impressed as I listened to the other poets all from different walks of life, passionately speaking their hearts in a language other than their own. I was in exaltation as I watched Zipporah take her turn. The power of her presence and words demanded the attention of every single ear in that room. I believe that this may have been some of their first times witnessing a powerful black queen perform spoken word live. I enjoyed the listeners' captivation as much as I enjoyed Zipporah's poem. After she finished the first round everyone was speechless. She received a score of eighty-nine out of one hundred, placing her third for the first round. The second round only consisted of the top five participants from the first round. This was getting heavy and my anxiety began to rise in the most exhilarating way. Zipporah made it to the second round! We all applauded her with pride and excitement, encouraging her that she has this in her hand. We took a short intermission and in ten minutes proceeded to the second and final round. I remember all five performers doing exceptionally well. Zipporah performed one of my favorite poems that she wrote called "Crying Queen." It artistically yet aggressively addresses the pain and experience of a black woman living in

America, enduring the negative lashes of a horrid history leaking into a confusing future. To be honest, I felt that one of the judges was offended by the poem's message and gave Zipporah a low score. There was another male poet who was powerful and authentic, but he unfortunately went over time, losing various points off his score. This gave Zipporah an advantage as he was the last performer. Zipporah possessed the highest score among those who had already performed. Spiritually and psychologically, she won without competition. But, by rule of the poetry slam, Zipporah walked away the first-place winner with the highest score. She performed well with memorization, did not stumble over words and remained within the time permitted. There was something very satisfying about witnessing Zipporah win this entire poetry slam in spite of the "offended judge." I rejoiced in my heart at this accomplishment. For it was not just hers, but it was all of ours to share. As a prize Zipporah received a voucher to eat at a well-known organic Greek restaurant. The founder of the poetry slam was so amazed by Zipporah that he made a phone call to the owner of the restaurant, insisting we all eat free and not just the Zipporah. We were so appreciative. We said our goodbyes, promising to return and quickly left to make it there before it closed. When we arrived, the place was packed with people. The owner greeted us with congratulations and seated us at a table already prepared for four. We took pictures with the owner and enjoyed the food. Every bite was delicious, and it was overall a beautiful experience. I was so proud of my sister that I almost cried. I could tell that this was only the tip of the iceberg when it came to our gifts and talents being shared with the world.

That iceberg was surely tipped when Zipporah was invited to perform at an open mic event in Madrid. This particular event was themed Black Joy as Resistance, inspired by the photo book titled *Black Joy and Resistance* by Adreinne Waheed. This event was very special to us because it was a commemoration of Black History Month. Who would have known that we would find an open mic celebrating our black history all the way in Spain? This affair was held by a black-owned organization called Art Spoken Madrid. This organization provided a platform here in Spain where people of color can express their artistry. Mr. Charles Snyder, the creative director and founder of this organization, made it enticing for us to attend the event. He was professional, informative and encouraging. He worked diligently to get as many melanated people as possible to this event to share the power of black talent and unity. Zipporah did not hesitate to submit her entry and purchase her ticket to Madrid. Amos and I felt it was a must for us to join as well. We wanted and needed this exposure of black love in Spain. So, we purchased our tickets as well.

"You should perform too, sis," Zipporah subtly suggested.

I could hear her spirit challenging and encouraging mine.

"The theme is Black Joy as Resistance," she stated with eagerness.

How ironic, I thought to myself as I went deep into reflection, simultaneously forming a poem in my head.

"I will, sissy, thank you!" I declared.

Many things went without saying between my sister and me because we were so in tune with each other. We all made preparations to leave for Madrid. Amos and I hired Tia Patri to watch the children for the weekend while we joined Zipporah for this spectacular experience. Zipporah arrived before us on a Friday morning. She wanted to meditate, relax and cook a meal for us before leaving for the event. Amos and I met her at the Airbnb later that evening. Upon our arrival we were greeted by Zipporah with good music, a delicious aroma and a cozy room ready for us. We walked into the beautiful and elegant apartment in amazement. By the look on the outside of the building, we were not sure what to expect from the inside. Nevertheless, we were surprised and relieved to see the total opposite. The place posed a home vibration with many beautiful paintings on the wall. The rooms were updated as well as the kitchen. All appliances worked perfectly well and both restrooms were sparkling clean. Zipporah had the table set for the three of us as it seemed to be a feast. There was homemade flat-noodle spaghetti accompanied with freshly sliced avocados, fried oyster mushrooms and fresh Spanish croissants. We all ate until we were stuffed, then got dressed to go out. The Black History event was scheduled for Saturday night. Zipporah being the party animal that she is found an R&B rooftop party in the city. This was a treat for us all because R&B was not a common music genre in the country of Spain as it is in the United States. It was held at the club of a five-star hotel called Hotel Puerta America Madrid. The hotel had a skyscraper that overlooked the Prosperidad neighborhood of Madrid. All three of us enjoyed listening to our old-school 1990's R&B jams. We all danced until the party ended then went back to the apartment to sleep and prepare for the big day.

I practiced my poem over and over, nervous to perform. I was honored to be a part of this event for it was a representation of myself and my people. The next morning Zipporah and I rested in preparation for our performance that evening. After we had breakfast, Amos decided to tour as much of the city as he possibly could. He saw impromptu street performers. He saw the beautiful palace of the king and queen of Spain. He thoroughly enjoyed the scenery alone with his camera in hand capturing every moment. When he returned, we all got dressed in our best African attire, ate a small snack and headed to the event. It was again, only less than a five-minute walk.

We arrived a little early, in time to meet Charles and his team. We laughed and socialized with so many other melanated individuals, which was uplifting and refreshing. To my observation, the coordinator of the Arts Spoken Madrid organization, Charles is a great man with a powerful vision. This event was proof of that power and vision. As we walked into the restaurant, we were directed downstairs into a dimly lit showroom. There was a very intimate stage with instruments on one side and the stage entrance on the other. Toward the back was a nice bar and small kitchen for drinks and refreshments. In front of the stage were tables and chairs positioned elegantly for the guests. The room was spacious yet intimate. It was full of beautiful black, brown, and white people of all diasporas! Some were dressed to impress, while others dressed casually. Seeing a large room full of melanin lifted and encouraged our spirits more than we realized. Charles and his team briefed all of the performers as we all began to prepare. The visual team was ready, musicians in place and Charles was pumped.

Out of eleven performers, Zipporah had the strategic honor of opening up the event. Charles asked her to go first because he felt that she was seasoned and a strong performer. This tactic displayed his expertise in the field. I was the fifth performer. Both my sister and I were super honored and excited to be able to perform at such a monumental movement. Amos was by my side, supporting me every step of the way. The people arrived all on time and took their seats. The room was packed with people from all around the world, all sharing the same desire to be elevated with love, talent and passion from each performer. Charles opened the event with a mighty introduction of the event's theme. When he introduced Zipporah, my heart began to beat fast in pride. I could feel Amos's nerves twitching as he wanted her to represent us well. I had no doubt that she would. Zipporah stepped on stage with a beautiful introduction of herself. She was so confident and unbothered. The first powerful poem that she recited was "Death to Life," a piece expounding on the need of our people to wake up and rise above the hatred and racism in this world. It captured the hearts of some while others were perplexed. Poetry can often have that effect on people. Her second poem that she recited was "Joyful Resistance." This was my favorite because it was a poem she wrote specifically for this event. I was amazed at her ability to memorize something so deep and profound in such a short time. Overall, Zipporah executed her performance and surely represented our tribe well. She ended the poem with a fist in the air, representing black strength and unity. Her performance was unforgettable as she set the tone with great competence. This was my second time seeing my sister perform live and I was flabbergasted. I was prouder of this performance than her win in Barcelona! It was something more special and supernatural about her pouring into the psyches of our beautiful black kings and queens in that room. Amos and I had smiles on our faces and satisfaction in our bones. As the event continued so did my nervousness.

I performed my poetry in the past but only during deployments and other military functions, which were many years ago. I realized that this was my first time performing at an open mic outside of the military and church. I can remember expressing my fear to Zipporah as she combatted it with her encouraging words. She was an expert and knew the feeling of nervousness before a performance. She gave me the best piece of advice that calmed my nerves.

"Just perform calmly as though you are conversing with them. Speak to your audience, sis!"

Her words rang through my head as I stood on the dark stage with the bright light hindering my view. I could feel my heart racing in my chest. I introduced myself with nerves in my voice. Then I stopped, took a deep breath and looked down to position my performance stance. I slowly raised my head and began to slowly recite my first poem ever written through memory. When the first line of my poem left my mouth, the calmness arrived, and my nervousness vanished without a trace. I was simply speaking to my audience who then imaginatively became my comforters and therapists. The silent sighs and acclamations of agreement could only be experienced in a room full of melanin. Every word oozing from the core of my heart.

Then, before I knew it, I completed my first and original poem: "My Black Pride."

There is something very special that I hold deep inside.
And that special something is my black pride.
It is an abstract feeling that burns within my heart.
It is a place near my soul, that is set apart.
Sometimes I think that my pride is too much,
and that I built it into a shield that no one can touch.
My mind stops and wonders how far my people came.
And what such a difference and influence we made.
Those history books are not going to tell you that America we helped build.
And that our strength and courage are made of steel.
when I think about my great-great-grandpa, who was a slave.
All the turmoil and toil he worked until his grave.
Oh, how much my great-great-grandpa must have suffered much misery and pain.
Then I look at myself and my family and realize that it was not in vain.
"Negro Spirituals" the slaves did sing.
Martin Luther King said, "Let freedom reign!"
And as a result, unity they did bring.
So, I obtain every right to have black pride.
Black history is the groom, and I am the bride.
So, if there is any feeling in me that will not shake.
A powerful feeling that will never break.
It is a powerful source that I will never let slip aside.
And that powerful source is my black pride.

        (Joy E. Glenn, "My Black Pride")

I barely heard the loud claps, cheers and finger snaps because I was focused and in a zone. I paused for a few moments and slowly read my second and most recent poem from my cellphone: "I Love My Melanin."

I love my dark brown skin that can absorb and receive healing from the sun.
I love my thick black hair, each loc representing my life journeys.
I love my voice, strong and containing a certain bass that produces both power and intimidation.
I love my spirit, in which I am always able to tap into God's presence.
I love my blood, which is permanently ingrained with God's DNA.
I love my strength, which can never be diminished no matter how many generations of abuse and hatred that we have endured.
I love my "offspring," who are already inevitably better versions of myself.
I love my king, who saw the queen in me and challenged her to come forth.
I love my life; a beautiful brown queen, living in a foreign land that unknowingly lavishes us with reverence.
And I love my name, JOY; given to me by depressed parents eager to break their generational curses.
Joy has been the source of my strength through my horrible past.
Now joy is what I possess as I walk my path of light.
My God, my melanin and my joy are all wrapped into one source of energy.
Me.
I love my melanin.

(Joy E. Glenn, "I Love My Melanin")

I strategically took a deep breath after each line, allowing my words and feelings to sink into the hearts and minds of my listeners. Suddenly, I was reciting the last line of my second poem. A wave of confidence and relief instantly rushed through my body. Without any deliberate thought, I blew a kiss to my audience and quickly yet confidently exited the stage. I was so proud of myself and so was my husband and sister. She gave me a standing ovation as others followed her. She screamed at the top of her lungs, eyes watering and clapping obnoxiously loud. She was proud of her baby sister and I felt it. Amos's smile warmed my heart, and his hug and kiss softened my nerves. I received various handshakes, encouraging words and love from the audience. We continued to watch amazing artists sharing their gifts and talents with us. Other Black American poets, Afro-Cubano drummers, singers and guitarist all made this night phenomenal. Words could not describe the vibration and healing that we all received from that night. Many performances uplifted us while others made us cry. All ministering to our hearts in different ways.

After the show we met and spoke to many different beautiful black people from the United States to the Caribbean to the United Kingdom and more. This was an amazing feeling! Shortly afterward, we walked about three miles to an Ethiopian restaurant that was recommended to us by a local woman who was vegan. Both the food and customer service were great. It was a perfect way to end the night. With full hearts and bellies we tipped the server and left the restaurant in good spirits. The next morning, we caught an early flight back to Utrera. But we basked from the beauty of that experience in Madrid for the rest of that month, hoping to encounter an event like that in our future.

Chapter 6:

Would I Stay?

During my entire three years of living in Spain, I am approached with the same question. Will I stay in Spain? This may seem like an easy question to answer, but it is not. My family and I have experienced much greatness and enjoyment while living in Spain, but do we want to call this our home for the next decade until the children are grown …? I believe it to be common for parents to possess the desire to obtain that perfect place to raise their children. However, some parents feel it necessary for their children to travel throughout their youth, living and learning through real, live escapades. Amos and I are the parents who want our children to grow up with friends they can call family. This is a characteristic of Utrera I truly adore. There is an innumerable number of people living in this town who have known each other for the majority of their lives. When I see Tina and her friends of over fifteen years, sharing stories of childhood memories, I think to myself, I want my children to have those same episodes of growing up with their best friends. Yet, when

I think of my children being raised in Utrera, I become a little weary. In my opinion, I believe my children, husband, sister and I would flourish more in a larger city. A city that embodies diversity, understanding of cultural differences and acceptance of change. I can honestly say that I would remain in Spain, but not in Utrera. This town was a great new beginning for us all and we will forever be grateful. Nevertheless, when the cons outweigh the pros, I would imagine that it is time to evolve and accept change. Therefore, when I am asked will I stay, I respond with yes. I would stay and raise my children in this beautifully imperfect country. Visualizing this change we are about to embark upon brings me gratitude and peace. It is within these moments that I envision the place we can all call home. Out of the many cities we have visited I would have to admit that Cadiz and Malaga are two of our favorite choices. We want our children to grow up near the ocean where all elements can be found. We want our lives to be not only rich but also fulfilling. I need my children to be comfortable in who they are, not only through the love for myself and them, but I also want them to find that love through themselves by seeing it in others. I believe that Utrera is not the place for my young black children to find that self-love. In my heart I can concur that this place I speak of, is within our reach. It is not just a goal, but it is our future. A bright future where we can feel accepted, genuinely loved, lacking the notion of being out of place. As a Black American woman, living in the United States for the majority of my life, I must admit that I honor and cherish diversity. I believe this is an important aspect of home placement. For it is not about the color of a skin, but it is about the sharing and respect of various beliefs, cultures and traditions. When one finds an ambience, which introduces a life full of change, growth and heterogeneity, one has found home. We have not currently found our home, but soon we will say differently.

From August of 2018 to this present day in the year 2021, I can say that my life in Spain has been very inspiring. Not only did I find my peace while living gracefully in Utrera, Spain, but I have also defeated anxiety and depression. Now don't get me wrong, I do not give sole credit for my life changes to one country. For that credit also belongs to God and me. Nonetheless, with its fresher foods, happier atmosphere, and lively culture, in Spain is where many loads have been lifted.

Small incidences of acceptance occasionally occurred. I can recall when I was approached by Cristina: one of the parents of Aaron's class. She asked if I could assist with the dance moves for the final play of the year. I obliged as I was honored to hear that she heard about my dancing skills from the other mothers attending our dance class. As we began preparation, Cristina volunteered to have the meetings at her house. She was ready to help and always available. I walked to Cristina's house because walking through the streets of this quaint town helps me feel tranquility and calmness. Upon my arrival, before entering Cristina's home I was greeted by two other parents, Ángeles and Loli. As I approached them, they both stopped talking and greeted me. Ángeles slowly gazed at me from head to toe. She smiled at me with a genuine kindness.

"What's up with you, Joy?" she asked with a slight undertone in her voice trickled with sarcasm. I was extremely amused by her gesture because it reminded me of home. I felt as though

Ángeles was one of my "homegirls from the block," her voice sounding like the voice of a "sister." I laughed to myself as I responded with humor.

"Nothing much, girl, just hanging in there."

Ángeles and Loli chuckled at my response as they heard my determination to speak Spanish the Andalusian way. As we exchanged a quick conversation about our children and my desire to stay in Spain, I realized that their comfort level with me was more relaxed. I felt they perceived that my family and I are here to stay, so that created a certain level of acceptance.

Each moment I discuss the lack of diversity in Utrera with Zipporah, I am often hit in the face with that same diversity. Yet, it is a researched fact that out of 52,000 people counted in the town of Utrera, only 667 are of other nationalities. We can only guess how many of those 667 are black. Nevertheless, Zipporah, Amos and I have met other men and women of color in this town—some from Latin America, others from the United States and Africa. I can recollect the day that I met my friend Beatrice, a strong and beautiful Afro-Columbian mother from Salesianos. Betty is married to a local Utreran. Together, they have three children. When I initially met Betty, her first child, Cristian, was twenty years old. Their daughter, Carolina, was nine years of age like my son Amari. Their youngest child was two. Within that schoolyear, we became friends. Our children became acquainted as well. Betty is beautiful, strong, prideful and bossy. My sister and I love her because she is fearless and proud. The year prior when we first arrived, Betty seemed unfriendly and uninterested. But, as time passed, Betty and I began to see more of each other through passing. We would speak more each day.

One morning we struck up a small conversation and exchanged numbers. However, it was not until nearly a year later that we finally made plans to have coffee. The first time that we met, we instantly made a beautifully natural connection. It was as though we had been friends for a while. What I noticed and loved most about Betty was the way that she carried herself. She would always walk upright with her head held high. This made me notice the times when I would walk with my head down as I would often fall into deep thought. But, because of my observation, I now ensure I am walking the way that I feel ... PROUD. Betty settled down in Utrera during her twenty-year marriage with her Spanish husband, Ramón. His spirit was gentle, and he was very nonchalant. Although there was an age gap between them, there seemed to be no gap in their genuine love and friendship with one another. This was evident when we went out with them one night and had a marvelous time.

Cristian, their twenty-one-year-old son, is a handsome, gentle, kindhearted, intelligent and powerful young man. However, to my discernment, Cristian did not know his worth. His spirit seemed to be friendly yet layered with insecurity, a little sadness and anxiety. Recognizing this about him caused me to ask him about his experience and upbringing in Utrera. I quickly realized that young Cristian was mending his spirit that had been damaged by his past. He experienced discrimination and hate as a young boy. He was attacked and mistreated by his peers throughout his school years. Simply because he was a brown boy with an Afro-Columbian mother and a European Spanish father. His unique qualities caused children to treat him unjustly. His father being a European and Utreran did not matter to his young attackers. They treated him differently because he was different. I saw the eyes of my young black children through his pain and wondered was this town for us. Perhaps the children were curious, intimidated, scared, ignorant, jealous or all of the above. Nevertheless, his truth was that he had residue of emotional, psychological and spiritual damage from these experiences. This saddened me. To see a young brown man so weighted down by insecurities, lacking the pride he should be carrying instead. This made my heart break as I wanted to witness to his soul. Nevertheless, I could sense his artistic abilities, so I then asked about his hobbies. Cristian confirmed my suspicion when he told me that he was indeed an artist. Intrigued, I asked to see some of his work. What I saw was alluring artwork. He is so talented! I thought to myself. I tried my best to explain to him that he must dig into his heart and embrace his Afro-Latin roots. I elaborated to Cristian that even though he was raised in Spain with a European father, it is important that he understand all aspects of his life. I encouraged him to explore his Afro-Columbian lineage. I believed much of his depression stemmed from his lack of knowledge for his complete self. "Unexplored self-territory" is what I have named it. Nonetheless, I could see the future of young Cristian becoming brighter as he evolves and learns more about himself. This interaction between Cristian and I gave me great perspective on my own life and the life of my three small children living in this small town of Spain.

Carolina is the nine-year-old daughter of Betty and Ramon. She is very beautiful, energetic and feisty just like her mother. She has long, thick, curly dark brown hair. I have never seen hair this lovely in my life. At a young age, she too possessed a sense of pride. However, her behavior and attitude were very typical of a young Andalusian girl: mature, feisty, prissy and energetic. I liked talking to her because her pride and confidence made me think of Abi, my baby girl. Their two-year-old daughter was very young, quiet, cute and shy. Being the same age as Abi I understood her behavior and knew how to communicate with her. I enjoyed getting to know Betty and her family as I hoped we would become more acquainted.

The relationships I have made while living in Utrera and visiting various cities in Spain have been a large encouragement to why I would stay in this country. I believe these connections are rare and unique. The few I call friends are those I would keep in my life for all eternity. Those that are not real and only for a moment will remain here in Utrera. For all relationships that come into our lives are experiences through which we are to learn and grow from. Whether family or friends, we all are present to teach, learn and continue to develop as humans on this earth.

When my oldest sister, Keturah, arrived with her wife, Meli Rosa, I felt the unity of my family not only develop, but we were expanding through love and common goals. D'iona's mother, my oldest sister, has endured many obstacles in her life. Nevertheless, she remains standing as she searches for the best opportunity for her and her family. She has always played a great role in my inspiration, and that is a reason why I chose to take D'iona along on this journey with us to Spain, as I was thinking of the future of our family as a whole.

Remembering the pain of my past and all the struggles of my people in America encourage my decision to choose happiness, honor and truth over patriotism. I will not lie and write that Spain will be the last place my family and I reside. But I can confidently profess that this country is a great option where my husband and I can raise our three beautiful children. Hoping that all of our family joins us on our passage to find home, we continue to actively search for the best city and home that fits the needs and desires of the entire tribe.

Keturah and Meli were making plans and preparation to move to Spain for about two months prior to their arrival. Keturah truly missed her daughter, D'iona, and needed to be reunited with her. When they finally arrived in Spain on a Wednesday night, I was ecstatic and couldn't wait to see my big sister. I was also anxious to meet Meli Rosa. The next morning, they came to my house before school started to surprise D'iona. First Zipporah walked into the gate as Keturah and Meli followed. When D'iona first laid eyes on her mother she gasped and screamed in surprise. They hugged one another tightly like Celie and Nettie in *The Color Purple*. As they continued their embrace, we all stood smiling quietly as we spectated. We then all walked the children to school. I was able to introduce Keturah and Meli to some of the friends Zipporah and I have made in Utrera. Within two weeks, Keturah and Meli found their own place in town near the school Salesianos. It was perfect and I knew that they both were anxious to start their lives together with D'iona.

As time progressed so did the hearts of Keturah and her wife. As did I, Keturah and Meli missed home. They both expressed their dislike for the particular habits of the Spaniards here. Keturah and Meli wanted to live in a more diverse city, not a small town. Their first option was Seville. Meli Rosa, being a Honduran woman, could understand and speak Spanish fluently. For her, there posed no struggle in communicating and understanding the people in Spain. After many days and weeks of searching, Keturah and Meli felt it would be best to return to the United States. Meli concluded that she disliked some of the rudeness and silly jokes some Spaniards made toward her and her wife. She felt that Utrera was rooted in racism and prejudices. Because we do not understand the language, we are missing many words of disrespect and incomprehension, she expressed. This made me feel sad that Meli felt this way, yet grateful to know her perspective. It was not until two years had passed living in this town, did I realize that Meli Rosa's observation carried some truth. Yet, in my opinion her truth was rooted in the scrutiny of her negativity. Therefore, my family and I have not experienced as much of the racism and prejudice as she and my sister did in just two months. However, it was presented to us at times during certain circumstances. Be that as it may, we also encountered other instances where the people in Utrera embraced us with care and appreciation.

We have had great experiences and delightful connections. For example, I can recall the day of Aaron's sixth birthday. This was during the time of COVID-19, when we all were quarantined. Every evening the people would stand outside of their homes applauding the essential workers of the town. We all appreciated the sacrifices they made every day to keep the town moving. It was a beautiful sight to see. This particular evening our neighbors surprised my baby boy with the sweetest gesture on his birthday. Aaron and I decided to venture upstairs to the terrace to get a better view as we socialized. When I opened the terrace door leading to outside there stood our neighbors to the left and the right, singing "Happy Birthday" to Aaron. Tears formed in my eyes as I watched María Del Mar and her family retrieve a homemade cake from inside their house with a number six candle on top. Aaron's face radiated with joy and gratification as he blew out his candle. My neighbors and I clapped for Aaron as the music blasted from across the street. We all laughed at the sight of Aaron's happy dance. His feet moving side to side with his little arms waving in the sky.

"Thank you very much," I expressed while holding back my emotions.

This one moment gave me a sense of grace and honor. Although I know this is not the home for our future, experiences such as this reminded by some of the people that this is our home for the present. With joy and peace in our hearts, we practice combatting any negative energy with positive energy. This is something I taught my son Amari to do while dealing with bullies. I know that this town is not perfect and I also know that a house is not a home without family love. We are a family of love, no matter what we may endure; for Psalm 30:5 states: "Weeping may endure for a night but joy cometh in the morning."

During the quarantine, we all witnessed a change in Aaron. In addition to his natural musical talent, his obsessions and ticks turned into artistry and gifts. I realized that Aaron has a photographic memory and an obsession with flags. He would sit at the table for hours drawing and coloring the flags of Spain, Andalusia and the United States of America. The intricate details of all flags were always present in his artwork. However, I realized his patriotism was stronger toward Spain than our own country. He always drew more flags of Spain. I concluded that his patriotism toward Spain equaled his appreciation of his growth here. We have watched this small shy toddler blossom into a super-intelligent courageous big boy.

Meanwhile, within two months of living in town, my sister and Meli decided that Spain itself was not for their family. They believed that D'iona and they would flourish better back in the United States. I honored their decision, even though I did not like it. I was sad to see D'iona and my sister go. Nonetheless, I stood in my humbleness and accepted this endeavor. Before Keturah and Meli left, Zipporah and I wanted to show them a good time in town. It was late Thursday night. We were all at Zipporah's house playing cards when she convinced us all to get dressed and go out. It was me, Zipporah, Keturah and Meli. Zipporah promised us that Utrera would be bursting with life and all the people would be at either Trece Bar or Antigua. These were two popular bars among the main crowd. However, it was after eleven at night when we went out and all we found were closed stores and empty bars with old men in them. Keturah, Meli and I laughed so hard at Zipporah.

"You dragged us all the way out here for a good time and this is what we get, Zipporah!?" Keturah teased as Meli and I both laughed.

"No, Keturah, this is rare! I swear normally it's popping on Thursday nights here!" Zipporah insisted.

"Sure it is," Keturah responded sarcastically.

We all continued to laugh.

We ended the night back at Zipporah's house talking and laughing. We enjoyed each other's company and ended the night in peace and positivity. Reminiscing on these times shared with Keturah, Meli Rosa and D'iona stimulated my desire to explore more of Spain. I soon realized that each person who visits Spain will not feel the same tranquil vibration as I do. This became a hard pill for me to swallow as I watched my sister and niece rapidly drift away from us all, mentally, spiritually and physically. They all left Spain at the end of the summer and didn't look back. I am proud to see my sister has her daughter back and has found love. Times with my family are very important to me as I strive to establish a place where we can unite in peace.

Many of our friends and relatives have come to visit, excited to say that they once took a vacation to Spain. Zipporah and I had a cousin Donesha come and visit for her thirty-first birthday. Our cousin Donesha or "Nene" was reaching a pivotal stage in her life and wanted to explore change. Both my sister and I were excited to share our lives and routines with Nene, showing her our lives in Spain. The first day she arrived we all went to a gathering at Rocio's family camp house. Before leaving for the evening gathering with the ladies, Zipporah and I ensured Nene was settled into her room. She secured her things in the house, freshened up and then we departed. We all, as usual, had a great time! Rocio and Tere introduced us to two other women present at the gathering. Both women were lovely and made us feel welcomed. The first woman we met was Laura. She is a sweet, fun and beautiful woman. She is also a single divorcee and mother of two beautiful daughters. Her older daughter, Laura, is a young teenager and very mature. I liked little Laura's energy because she seemed confident in who she is. This can be a very uncommon trait among teenagers. Laura also had a younger daughter, Lucia. Lucia was sweet and timid. Her spirit was kind and so was her personality as I noticed while she played with Abi and Aaron. They both played very well with my children and looked after them while the mothers socialized. The other woman we met was Mari Carmen, an equally beautiful, bright vibrant and welcoming woman. She was from a small town nearby called El Coronil, a town less than five miles away from where my husband worked. We all laughed, sang karaoke, danced, drank and ate good food. It was pleasant spending time with positive people. Mari Carmen had to leave early, and Amos came to get the children when they got tired. This gave me a little "adult time," which I was always appreciative to receive.

Cross-culturalization took place as we exchanged music and dance techniques. Zipporah and I loved watching traditional Andalusian flamenco dancing, and we watched Rocio show off her moves. In these moments we all seemed to feel the same energy of freedom. It was as if we were all little girls again playing, singing and dancing all night until the moon arrived. We were all comfortable enough with each other to let our guard down and show our vibrant and free sides. Rocio's mother made a beautiful display of unique foods, honoring us as foreign guests in her home. She brought out a beautiful traditional dish for Zipporah, our cousin Nene and me. It consisted of half an eggplant stuffed with ground chicken, onions, garlic, bell peppers and some other ingredients that I was not aware of. It was extremely delicious and we all three enjoyed it. As the moon continued to light up the night, Rocio played traditional flamenco music as she danced under the stars. We all watched, clapped and encouraged her form of art. Tere ended the night by sharing her beautiful view on relationships. She stated how all parties must make an effort to maintain our connections. We all agreed. It was days like this that made me feel that Utrera could be home for my family and me. Yet, there were also more situations that convinced me otherwise. Nonetheless, I will forever cherish these moments and hold on to the friendships sustained with true love and unity.

At the end of the night Nene expressed how she realized the difference in character of the people here in Spain, compared to those in America. Her observations were true, but that truth was geared toward the people whom Zipporah and I attracted. These women and their families were not representations of all people in Utrera. Nevertheless, Nene loved the freedom in the lives of the people. She also adored their family orientation. She equally admired our friends' pure acceptance of people from different countries and cultures. In spite of the language barrier, these women made every effort to proudly communicate their hospitality.

The next morning, the family took time to relax and catch up. Much-needed deep, spiritual and intellectual conversations transpired between Nene and me. During the evening, Amari, Nene and I took a stroll to the plaza for ice cream and ended the day with a family dinner at home. Each day I ensured Nene received the full experience of living in Spain. We walked to the Wednesday market, visited the city of Seville, experienced a wine tasting, ate dinner at a fine restaurant, watched live flamenco dancers and more. My cousin's time here was well spent, and she was grateful for every moment. I was proud of Donesha for stepping out of her comfort zone by obtaining her goal of traveling the world. Spain was just the beginning for our cousin and we looked forward to seeing her again.

One aspect of my life that I have always enjoyed, is people's willingness to share their stories with me. I love it even more now that we are living in Spain. Many people were happy to sit and share their culture and lives with me. And I feel that there is a mutual respect because they see that my family and I care. We want to learn and experience their culture and its entirety. I suppose my inquisitive mind and vivid imagination feel as though I am learning the southern culture of Spain as a whole. But I also get the extra privilege of peeking into the personal lives of many Spaniards from all over. Many of which I only met once and never saw again. Still, I felt that each individual had their own separate lives and separate amazing experiences. And every beautiful person that was open enough to share some of their personal lives with me played out in my head like a dramatic soap opera on television.

I realize that we have much more of Spain to explore, especially the northern regions with their own set of customs and traditions. All of our travel endeavors and interactions with Spaniards from all over this country have formed my opinions and conclusions. Thus, I can feel my queenly roots settling into the grounds of this beautiful country of Spain. But in Andalusia. As stated before, my family and I would like to stay in the South where the weather is warmer and so are the beaches.

My family and I equally enjoyed our visits to the larger and more urban cities like Madrid, Barcelona and Malaga. We relished in the evident diversity that each city possessed. I realize that no country is perfect and neither is life. But peace and joy can be found in the midst of it all. This was a very pivotal lesson that I learned over these past few years and our time here in Spain has proven it.

Overall, our experience here in Spain has been nothing short of a big, beautiful dream. The country of Spain is radiant in so many ways. Although most of our experiences have been in the province of Andalusia, I would not have wished for any other region. I feel comfortable to confess that I believe God strategically placed my family and me in one of the most cultural parts of Spain. While some endeavors here have been pleasant, others have not. However, we have learned to take the good with the bad as the vast majority of our interactions and experiences in Spain have been awesome. I believe that many people in Andalusia and Spain have openly embraced my family and me. At times, I could hear their hearts quietly whispering, "You and your family are all honored guests in our country. We will respect, teach, help and love you so long as you do the same for us and our culture." My family and I have openly accepted the blatant embrace yet challenge. Furthermore, I admit that Spain is the place where I settled into my complete healing, and for that I will always be grateful. For with that gratitude, we all can find a home here.

Chapter 7:

Spain Through the Eyes of my Camera Lens

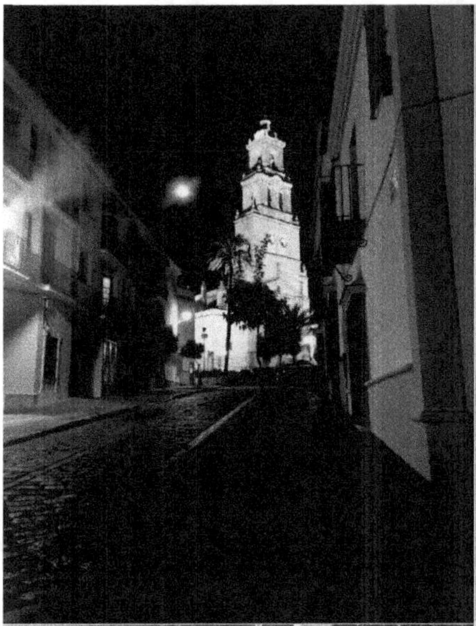

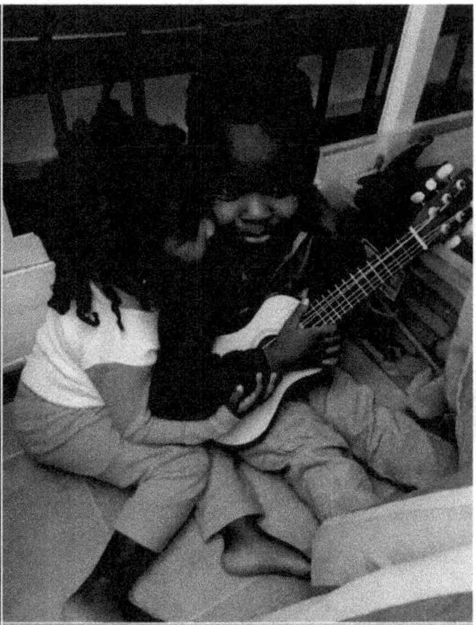

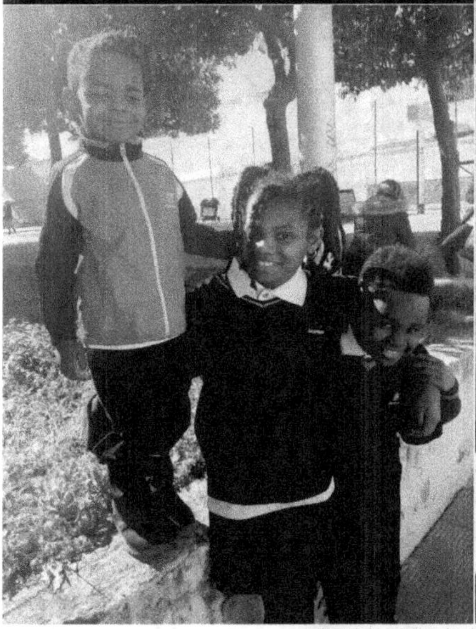

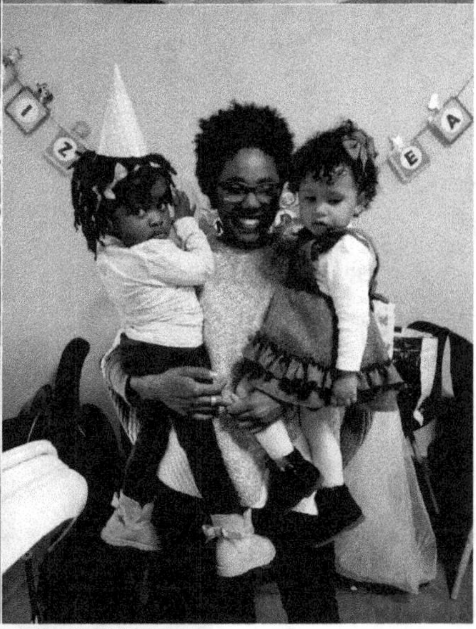

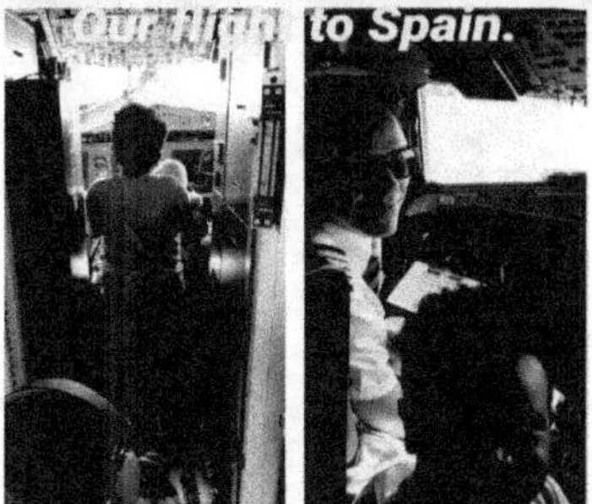
Our flight to Spain.

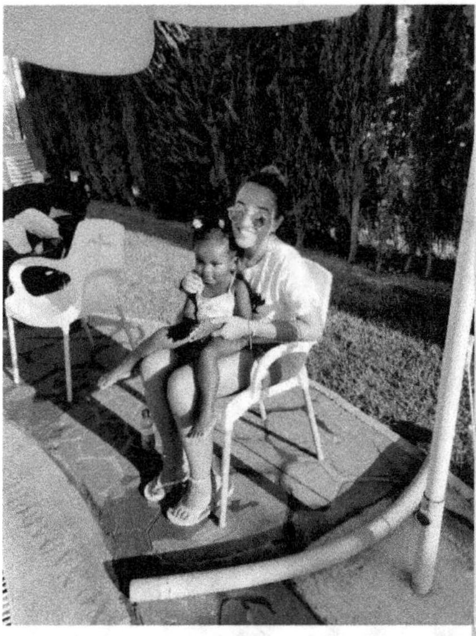

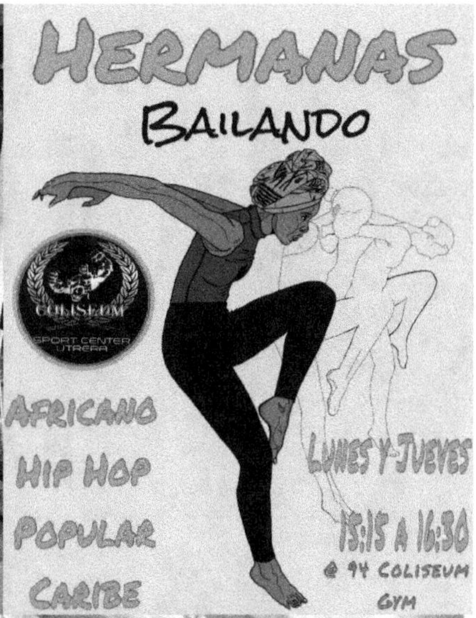
HERMANAS
BAILANDO
COLISEUM
SPORT CENTER
UTRERA
AFRICANO
HIP HOP
POPULAR
CARIBE
LUNES Y JUEVES
15:15 A 16:30
@ 94 COLISEUM
GYM

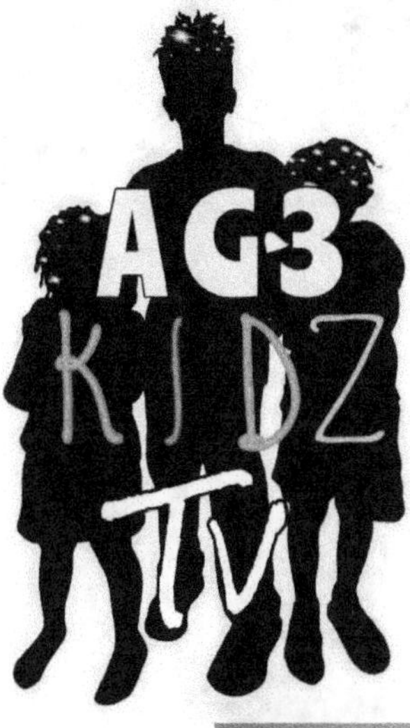
AG3
KIDZ
TV

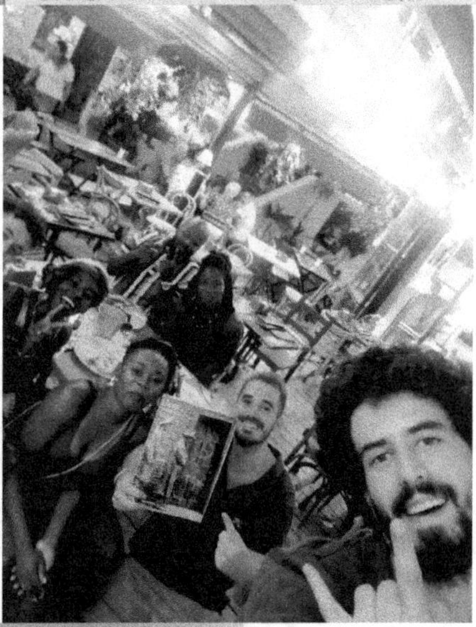

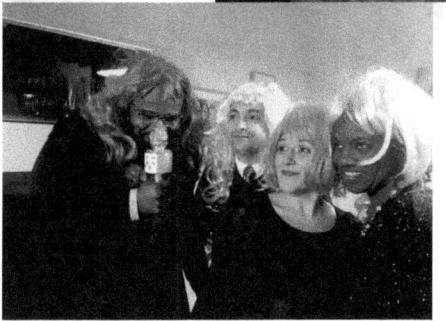

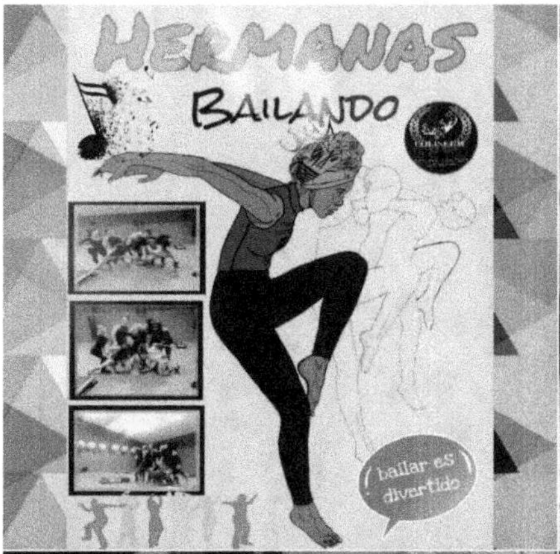
HERMANAS
BAILANDO
bailar es divertido
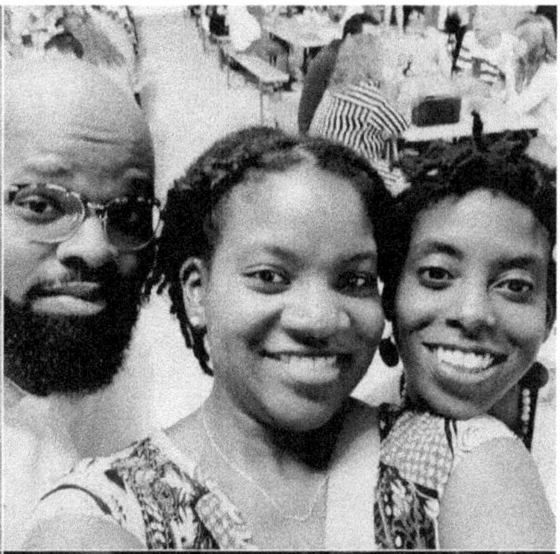
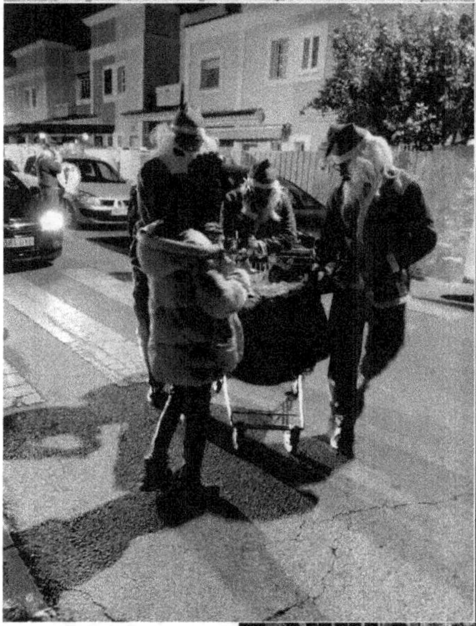
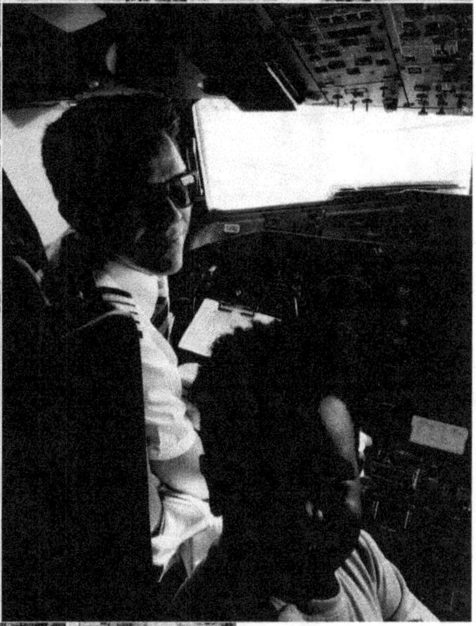

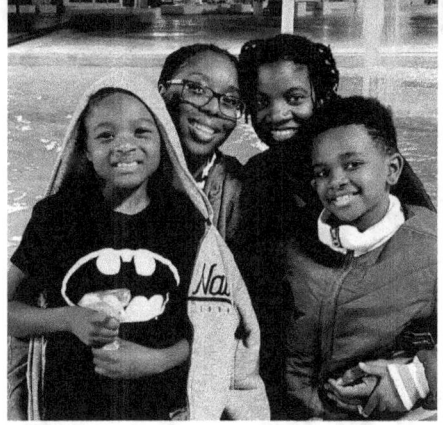

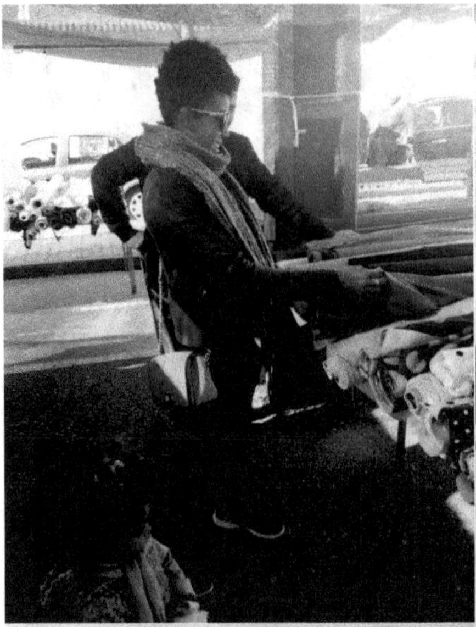

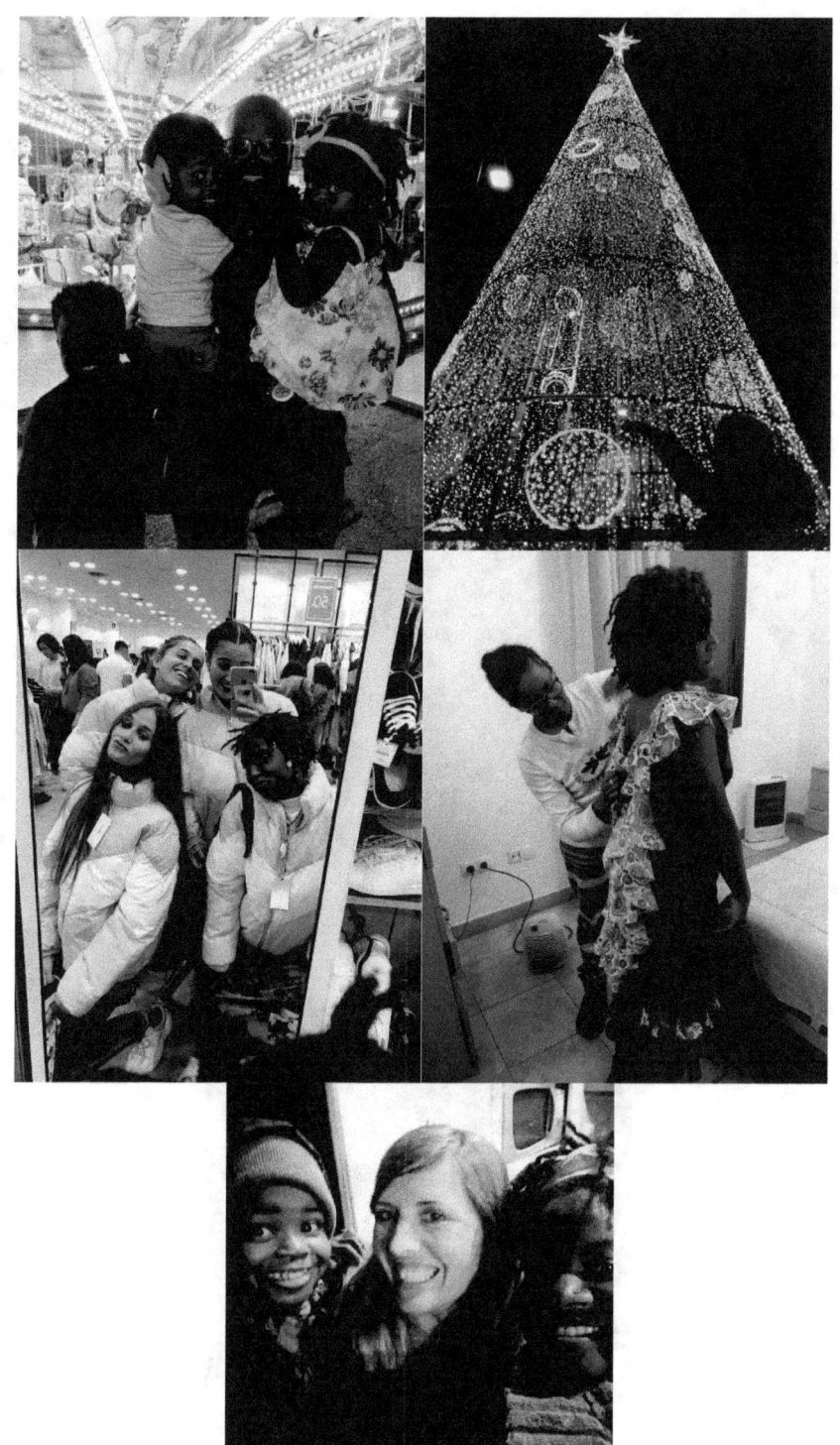

Photographed by Julián Novalbos Ruiz

Contact Page

To find out more about Joy Glenn please visit her following links:

www.authorjoyeglenn.com

YouTube Channel
https://www.youtube.com/channel/UCOIdc2v4S50LQR4dDrBqAwQ

Facebook:
https://www.facebook.com/authorjoye.glenn

Pinterest:
https://www.pinterest.com/

Twitter:
https://twitter.com/JoyEGlenn3

www.ingramcontent.com/pod-product-compliance
Lightning Source LLC
Chambersburg PA
CBHW072147100526
44589CB00015B/2127